I0101700

Pebbles *On The* Shore

Alfred George Gardiner

... collecting toys
And trifles for choice matters, worth a sponge;
As children gathering pebbles on the shore

Merchant Books
1916

Copyright © 2009 Merchant Books

ISBN 1-60386-254-4

DIGITALIZED BY
WATCHMAKER PUBLISHING
ALL RIGHTS RESERVED

Preface

These papers were begun as a part of a causerie in *The Star*, the other contributors to which—men whose names are household words in contemporary literature—wrote under the pen names of "Aldebaran," "Arcturus" and "Sirius." But the constellation, formed in the early days of the war, did not long survive the agitations of that event, and when "Arcturus" left for the battlefield it was finally dissolved and "Alpha of the Plough" alone remained to continue the causerie. This selection from his papers is a sort of informal diary of moods in a time of peril. They are pebbles gathered on the shore of a wild sea.

To
All Who Love
The Cottage In The
Beechwoods

Contents

On Choosing A Name   9

On Letter-Writing   12

On Reading In Bed   15

On Cats And Dogs   17

"W.G."   19

On Seeing Visions   22

On Black Sheep   25

The Village And The War   27

On Rumour   30

On Umbrella Morals   33

On Talking To One's Self   36

On Boswell And His Miracle   39

On Seeing Ourselves   42

On The English Spirit   45

On Falling In Love   48

On A Bit Of Seaweed   51

On Living Again   53

Tu-Whit, Tu-Whoo!   56

On Points Of View   59

On Beer And Porcelain   61

On A Case Of Conscience   64

On The Guinea Stamp   67

On The Dislike Of Lawyers   70

On The Cheerfulness Of The Blind   72

On Taxing Vanity   75

On Thoughts At Fifty   77

The One-Eyed Cat   80

On The Philosophy Of Hats   83

On Seeing London   85

On Catching The Train   87

In Praise Of Chess   90

On The Downs   93

On Short Legs And Long Legs   95

On A Painted Face   97

On Writing An Article   99

On A City That Was   101

On Pleasant Sounds   103

On Slackening The Bow   106

On The Intelligent Golf Ball   108

On A Prisoner Of War   110

On The World We Live In   113

"I'm Telling You"   116

On Courage   118

On Spendthrifts   121

On A Top Hat   123

On Losing One's Memory   126

On Wearing A Fur-Lined Coat   128

In Praise Of Walking   131

On Rewards And Riches   134

On Taste   137

On A Hawthorn Hedge   139

ON CHOOSING A NAME

"As for your name, I offer you the whole firmament to choose from." In that prodigal spirit the editor of the *Star* invites me to join the constellation that he has summoned from the vasty deeps of Fleet Street. I am, he says, to shine punctually every Wednesday evening, wet or fine, on winter nights and summer eves, at home or abroad, until such time as he cries: "Hold, enough!" and applies the extinguisher that comes to all.

The invitation reaches me in a tiny village on a spur of a range of beech clad hills, whither I have fled for a breathing space from the nightmare of the war and the menacing gloom of the London streets at night. Here the darkness has no terrors. In the wide arch of the sky our lamps are lit nightly as the sun sinks down far over the great plain that stretches at our feet. None of the palpitations of Fleet Street disturb us, and the rumours of the war come to us like far-off echoes from another world. The only sensation of our day is when, just after darkness has fallen, the sound of a whistle in the tiny street of thatched cottages announces that the postman has called to collect letters.

In this solitude, where one is thrown entirely upon one's own resources, one discovers how dependent one is upon men and books for inspiration. It is hard even to find a name. Not that finding a name is easy in any circumstances. Everyone who lives by his pen knows the difficulty of the task. I would rather write an article than find a title for it. The thousand words come easily (sometimes); but the five-words summary of the thousand, that is to flame at the top like a beacon light, is a gem that has to be sought in travail, almost in tears. I have written books, but I have never found a title for one that I have written. That has always come to me from a friend.

Even the men of genius suffer from this impoverishment. When Goldsmith had written the finest English comedy since Shakespeare he did not know what to call it, and had to leave Johnson to write the label. I like to think that Shakespeare himself suffered from this sterility—that he, too, sat biting the feather of his quill in that condition of despair that is so familiar to smaller men. Indeed, we have proof that it was so in the titles themselves. Is not the title, *As You Like It*, a confession that he had bitten his quill until he was tired of the vain search for a name? And what is *Twelfth Night* or *What You Will* but an evidence that he could not hit upon any name that would fit the most joyous offspring of his genius?

What parent does not know the same agony? To name a child, to give him a sign that shall go with him to his grave, and that shall fit that mystery of the cradle which time and temptation and trial shall alone reveal—*hoc opus, hic labor est*. Many fail by starting from false grounds—fashion, ambition, or momentary interest. Perhaps the little stranger arrives with the news of a battle, or when a popular novel appears, or at a moment when you are under the influence of some austere or heroic name. And forgetful that it is the child that has to bear the burden of your momentary impulse, you call him Inkerman Jones, or Kitchener Smith, or Milton Spinks.

And so he is started on his journey, like a little historical memory, or challenging comparison with some hero of fact or fable. Perhaps Milton Spinks grows up bow-legged and commonplace—all Spinks and no Milton. As plain John he would pass through life happy and unnoticed, but the great name of Milton hangs about him like a jest from which he can never escape—no, not even in the grave, for it will be continued there until the lichen has covered the name on the headstone with stealthy and kindly oblivion.

It is a good rule, I think, to avoid the fanciful in names. So few of our children are going to be heroes or sages that we should be careful not to stamp them with the mark of greatness at the outset of the journey. Horatio was a happy stroke for Nelson, but how few Horatios win immortality, or deserve it! And how disastrous if Horatio turns out a knave and a coward! If young Spinks has any Miltonic fire within him, it will shine through plain John more naturally and lustrously than through any borrowed patronymic. You may be as humble as you like, and John will fit you: as illustrious as you like, and John will blaze as splendid as your deeds, linking you with that great order of nobility of which John Milton, John Hampden, and John Bright are types.

I had written thus far when it occurred to me that I had still my own name to choose and that soon the whistle of the postman would be heard in the street. I went out into the orchard to take counsel with the stars. The far horizon was still stained wine-red with the last embers of the day; northward over the shoulder of the hill the yellow moon was rising full-orbed into the night sky and the firmament glittered with a thousand lamps.

How near and familiar they seem to one in the solitude of the country! In the town our vision is limited to the street. We see only the lights of the pavement and hear only the rattle of the unceasing traffic. The stars seem infinitely removed from our life.

But here they are like old neighbours for whom we never look in vain, intimate though eternal, friendly and companionable though far off. There is Orion coming over the hill, and there the many-jewelled Pleiades, and across the great central dome of the sky the vast triangle formed by the Pole Star, golden Arcturus (not now visible), and ice-blue Vega. But these are not names for me. Better are those homely sounds that link the pageant of night with the immemorial life of the fields. Arcturus is Alpha of the Herdsman. Shall it be that?

And then my eye roves westward to where the Great Bear hangs head downwards as if to devour the earth. Great Bear, Charles's Wain, the Plough, the Dipper, the Chariot of David—with what fancies the human mind through all the ages has played with that glorious constellation! Let my fancy play with it too. There at the head of the Plough flames the great star that points to the pole. I will hitch my little waggon to that sublime image. I will be Alpha of the Plough.

ON LETTER-WRITING

Two soldiers, evidently brothers, stood at the door of the railway carriage—one inside the compartment, the other on the platform.

"Now, you won't forget to write, Bill," said the latter.

"No," said Bill. "I shall be back at—tonight, and I'll write all round to-morrow. But, lor, what a job. There's mother and the missus and Bob and Sarah and Aunt Jane and Uncle Jim, and—well, you know the lot. You've had to do it, Sam."

"Yes," said Sam, ruefully; "it's a fair teaser."

"And if you write to one and miss another they're offended," continued Bill. "But I always mention all of 'em. I say 'love to Sarah,' and 'hope Aunt Jane's cold's better,' and that sort of thing, and that fills out a page. But I'm blowed if I can find anything else to say. I just begin 'hoping this finds you well, as it leaves me at present,' and then I'm done. What else is there to say?"

"Nothing," said Sam, mournfully. "I just sit and scratch my head over the blessed paper, but nothing'll come. Seems as though my head's as empty as a drum."

"Same here. 'Tisn't like writing love-letters. When I was up to that game 'twas easy enough. When I got stuck I just put in half a page of crosses, and that filled up fine. But writing to mother and the missus and Sarah and Jim and the rest is different. You can't fill up with crosses. It would look ridiklus."

"It would," said Sam.

Then the train began to move, and the soldier in the train sank back on his seat, took out a cigarette, and began to smoke. I found he had been twice out at the front, and was now home on sick leave. He had been at the battle of Mons, through the retreat to the Marne, the advance to the Aisne, the first battle of Ypres, and the fighting at Festubert. In a word, he had seen some of the greatest events in the world's history, face to face, and yet he confessed that when he came to writing a letter, even to his wife, he could find nothing to say. He was in the position of the lady mentioned by Horace Walpole, whose letter to her husband began and ended thus: "I write to you because I have nothing to do: I finish because I have nothing to say."

I suppose there has never been so much letter-writing in the world as is going on to-day, and much of it is good writing, as the papers show. But the case of my companion in the train is the case of thousands and tens of thousands of young fellows who for the first time in their lives want to write and discover that they have no gift of self-expression. It is not that they are stupid. It is that somehow the act of writing paralyses them. They cannot condense the atmosphere in which they live to the concrete word. You have to draw them out. They need a friendly lead. When they have got that they can talk well enough, but without it they are dumb.

In the great sense letter-writing is no doubt a lost art. It was killed by the penny post and modern hurry. When Madame de Sévigny, Cowper, Horace Walpole, Byron, Lamb, and the Carlyles wrote their immortal letters the world was a leisurely place where there was time to indulge in the luxury of writing to your friends. And the cost of franking a letter made that letter a serious affair. If you could only send a letter once in a month or six months, and then at heavy expense, it became a matter of first-rate consequence. The poor, of course, couldn't enjoy the luxury of letter-writing at all. De Quincey tells us how the dalesmen of Lakeland a century ago used to dodge the postal charges. The letter that came by stage coach was received at the door by the poor mother, who glanced at the superscription, saw from a certain agreed sign on it that Tom or Jim was well, and handed it back to the carrier unopened. In those days a letter was an event.

Now when you can send a letter half round the globe for a penny, and when the postman calls half a dozen times a day, few of us take letter-writing seriously. Carlyle saw that the advent of the penny post would kill the letter by making it cheap. "I shall send a penny letter next time," he wrote to his mother when the cheap postage was about to come in, and he foretold that people would not bother to write good letters when they could send them for next to nothing. He was right, and the telegraph, the telephone, and the postcard have completed the destruction of the art of letter-writing. It is the difficulty or the scarcity of a thing that makes it treasured. If diamonds were as plentiful as pebbles we shouldn't stoop to pick them up.

But the case of Bill and Sam and thousands of their comrades to-day is different. They don't want to write literary letters, but they do want to tell the folks at home something about their life and the great things of which they are a part. But the great things are too great for them. They cannot put them into words. And they ought not to try, for the secret of letter-writing is intimate triviality. Bill could not have described the retreat from Mons; but he could have told, as he told me, about the blister he got on his heel, how he hungered for a smoke, how he marched and marched until he fell asleep marching, how he lost his pal at Le Cateau, and how his boot sole dropped off at Meaux. And through such trivialities he would have given a living picture of the great retreat.

In short, to write a good letter you must approach the job in the lightest and most casual way. You must be personal, not abstract. You must not say, "This is too small a thing to put down." You must say, "This is just the sort of small thing we talk about at home. If I tell them this they will see me, as it were, they'll hear my voice, they'll know what I'm about." That is the purpose of a letter. Keats expresses the idea very well in one of those voluminous letters which he wrote to his brother George and his wife in America and in which he poured out the wealth of family affection which was one of the most amiable features of his character. He has described how he had been to see his mother, how she had laughed at his bad jokes, how they went out to tea at Mrs. Millar's, and how in going they were struck with the light and shade through the gateway at the

Horse Guards. And he goes on: "I intend to write you such volumes that it will be impossible for me to keep any order or method in what I write; that will come first which is uppermost in my mind, not that which is uppermost in my heart–besides I should wish to give you a picture of our lives here whenever by a touch I can do it; even as you must see by the last sentence our walk past Whitehall all in good health and spirits–this I am certain of because I felt so much pleasure from the simple idea of your playing a game of cricket."

There is the recipe by one of the masters of the craft. A letter written in this vein annihilates distance; it continues the personal gossip, the intimate communion, that has been interrupted by separation; it preserves one's presence in absence. It cannot be too simple, too commonplace, too colloquial. Its familiarity is not its weakness, but its supreme virtue. If it attempts to be orderly and stately and elaborate, it may be a good essay, but it will certainly be a bad letter.

ON READING IN BED

Among the few legacies that my father left me was a great talent for sleeping. I think I can say, without boasting, that in a sleeping match I could do as well as any man. I can sleep long, I can sleep often, and I can sleep sound. When I put my head on the pillow I pass into a fathomless peace where no dreams come, and about eight hours later I emerge to consciousness, as though I have come up from the deeps of infinity.

That is my normal way, but occasionally I have periods of wakefulness in the middle of the night. My sleep is then divided into two chapters, and between the chapters there is a slab of unmitigated dreariness. It is my hour of pessimism. The tide has ebbed, the water is dead-low, and there is a vista of endless mud. It is then that this tragi-comedy of life touches bottom, and I see the heavens all hung with black. I despair of humanity, I despair of the war, I despair of myself. There is not one gleam of light in all the sad landscape, and the abyss seems waiting at my feet to swallow me up with everything that I cherish. It is no use saying to this demon of the darkness that I know he is a humbug, a mere Dismal Jemmy of the brain, who sits there croaking like a night owl or a tenth-rate journalist. My Dismal Jemmy is not to be exorcised by argument. He can only be driven out by a little sane companionship.

So I turn on a light and call for one of my bedside friends. They stand there in noble comradeship, ready to talk, willing to remain silent, only asking to do my pleasure. Oh, blessed be the name of Gutenberg, the Master Printer. A German? I care not. Even if he had been a Prussian—which I rejoice to think he was not—I would still say: "Blessed be the name of Gutenberg," though Sir Richard Cooper, M.P., sent me to the Tower for it. For Gutenberg is the Prometheus not of legend but of history. He brought down the sacred flame and scattered the darkness that lay on the face of the waters. He gave us the *Daily Owl*, it is true, but he made us also freemen of time and thought, companions of the saints and the sages, sharers in the wisdom and the laughter of the ages. Thanks to him I can, for the expenditure of a few shillings, hear Homer sing and Socrates talk and Rabelais laugh; I can go chivvying the sheep with Don Quixote and roaming the hills with Borrow; I can carry the whole universe of Shakespeare in my pocket, and call up spirits to drive Dismal Jemmy from my pillow.

Who are these spirits? In choosing them it is necessary to avoid the deep-browed argumentative fellows. I do not want Plato or Gibbon or any of the learned brotherhood by my bedside, nor the poets, nor the novelists, nor the dramatists, nor even the professional humorists. These are all capital fellows in their way, but let them stay downstairs. To the intimacy of the bedside I admit only the kindly fellows who come in their dressing-gowns and slippers, so to speak, and sit down and just talk to you as though they had known you ever since you were a little nipper, and your father and your grandfather before you. Of course, there is old Montaigne. What a glorious gossip he is!

What strange things he has to tell you, what a noble candour he shows! He turns out his mind as carelessly as a boy turns out his pockets, and gives you the run of his whole estate. You may wander everywhere, and never see a board warning you to keep off the grass or reminding you that you are a trespasser.

And Bozzy. Who could do without Bozzy by his bedside–dear, garrulous old Bozzy, most splendid of toadies, most miraculous of reporters? When Bozzy begins to talk to me, and the old Doctor growls "Sir," all the worries and anxieties of life fall magically away, and Dismal Jemmy vanishes like the ghost at cock-crow. I am no longer imprisoned in time and the flesh: I am of the company of the immortals. I share their triumphant aloofness from the play that fills our stage and see its place in the scheme of the unending drama of men.

That sly rogue Pepys, of course, is there–more thumb-stained than any of them except Bozzy. What a miracle is this man who lives more vividly in our eyes than any creature that ever walked the earth! What was the secret of his magic? Is it not this, that he succeeded in putting down on paper the real truth about himself? A small thing? Well, you try it. You will find it the hardest job you have ever tackled. No matter what secrecy you adopt you will discover that you cannot tell yourself the *whole truth* about yourself. Pepys did that. Benvenuto Cellini pretended to do that, but I refuse to believe the fellow. Benjamin Franklin tried to do it and very nearly succeeded. St. Augustine was frank enough about his early wickedness, but it was the overcharged frankness of the subsequent saint. No, Pepys is the man. He did the thing better than it has ever been done in this world.

I like to have the *Paston Letters* at my bedside, too. Then I go off to sleep again in the fifteenth century with the voice of old Agnes Paston sounding in my ears. Dead half a thousand years, yet across the gulf of time I hear the painful scratching of her quill as she sends "Goddis blyssyng" to her son in London, and tells him all her motherly gossip and makes the rough life of far-off Tudor England live forever. Dear old Agnes! She little thought as she struggled with her spelling and her pen that she was writing something that was immortal. If she had known, I don't think she would have bothered. She was a very matter-of-fact old lady, and was too full of worries to have much room for vanities.

I should like to say more about my bedside friends–strapping George Borrow sitting with Petulengro's sister under the hedge or fighting the Flaming Tinman; the dear little Boston doctor who talks so chirpily over the Breakfast Table; the *Compleat Angler* that takes you out into an eternal May morning, and Sainte-Beuve whom I have found a first-rate bedside talker. But I must close.

There is one word, however, to be added. Your bedside friends should be dressed in soft leather and printed on thin paper. Then you can talk to them quite snugly. It is a great nuisance if you have to stick your arms out of bed and hold your hands rigid.

ON CATS AND DOGS

A friend of mine calling to see me the other day and observing my faithful Airedale—"Quilp" by name—whose tail was in a state of violent emotion at the prospect of a walk, remarked that when the new taxes came in I should have to pay a guinea for the privilege of keeping that dog. I said I hoped that Mr. McKenna would do nothing so foolish. In fact, I said, I am sure he will do nothing so foolish. I know him well, and I have always found him a sensible man. Let him, said I, tax us all fairly according to our incomes, but why should he interfere with the way in which we spend the money that he leaves us? Why should he deny the friendship of that most friendly animal the dog to a poor man and make it the exclusive possession of the well-to-do?

The emotion of Quilp's tail kept pace with the fervour of my remarks. He knew that he was the subject of the conversation, and his large brown eyes gleamed with intelligence, and his expressive eyebrows were eloquent of self-pity and appeal. He was satisfied that whatever the issue I was on his side, and at half a hint he would have given my friend a taste of the rough side of his tongue. But he is a well-mannered brute, and knows how to restrain his feelings in company.

What would be the result of your high tax? I continued with passion. It would be a blow at the democracy of dogs. It would reduce the whole of dogdom to a pampered class of degenerates. Is there anything more odious than the spectacle of a fat woman in furs nursing a lap dog in furs, too? It is as degrading to the noble family of dogs as a footman in gold buttons and gold braid is to the human family. But it is just these degenerates whom a high tax would protect. Honest fellows like Quilp here (more triumphant tail flourishes), dogs that love you like a brother, that will run for you, carry for you, bark for you, whose candour is so transparent and whose faithfulness has been the theme of countless poets—dogs like these would be taxed out of existence.

Now cats, I continued—(at the thrilling word Quilp became tense with excitement), cats are another affair. Personally I don't care two pence if Mr. McKenna taxes them a guinea a whisker. There is only one moment in the life of a cat that is tolerable, and that is when it is not a cat but a kitten. Who was the Frenchman who said that women ought to be born at seventeen and die at thirty? Cats ought to die when they cease to be kittens and become cats.

Cats, said my friend coldly, are the spiritual superiors of dogs. The dog is a flunkey, a serf, an underling, a creature that is eternally watching its master. Look at Quilp at this moment. What a spectacle of servility. You don't see cats making themselves the slaves of men. They like to be stroked, but they have no affection for the hand that strokes them. They are not parasites, but independent souls, going their own way, living their own lives, indifferent to applause, calling no man master. That is why the French consider them so superior to dogs.

I do not care what the French think, I said with warmth.

But they are our Allies, said my friend severely. The Germans, on the other hand, prefer dogs. I hope you are not a pro-German.

On the cat-and-dog issue I am, and I don't care who knows it, I said recklessly. And I hate these attempts to drag in prejudice. Moreover, I would beg you to observe that it was a great Frenchman, none other than Pascal, who paid the highest of all tributes to the dog. "The more I see of men," he said, "the better I like dogs." I challenge you to produce from any French source such an encomium on the cat.

No, I continued, the dog is a generous, warmhearted, chivalrous fellow, who will play with you, mourn for you, or die for you. Why, literature is full of his heroism. Who has climbed Helvellyn without being haunted by that shepherd's dog that inspired Scott and Byron? Or the Pass of St. Bernard without remembering the faithful hounds of the great monastery? But the cat is a secret and alien creature, selfish and mysterious, a Dr. Jekyll and Mr. Hyde. See her purring on the hearth-rug in front of the fire, and she seems the picture of innocence and guileless content. All a blind, my dear fellow, all a blind. Wait till night comes. Then where is demure Mistress Puss? Is she at home keeping vigil with the good dog Tray? No, the house may be in blazes or ransacked by burglars for all she cares. She is out on the tiles and in back gardens pursuing her unholy ritual—that strange ritual that seems so Oriental, so sinister, so full of devilish purpose. I can understand the old association of witchcraft with cats. The sight of cats almost makes me believe in witchcraft, in spite of myself. I can believe anything about a cat. She is heartless and mercenary. Her name has become the synonym of everything that is mean, spiteful, and vicious. "An old cat" is the unkindest thing you can say about a woman.

But the dog wears his heart on his sleeve. His life is as open as the day. He has his indecorums, but he has no secrets. You may see the worst of him at a glance, but the best of him is inexhaustible. A cat is as remote from your life as a lizard, but a dog is as intimate as your own thoughts or your own shadow, and his loyalty is one of the consolations of a disloyal world. You remember that remark of Charles Reade's: "He was only a man, but he was as faithful as a dog." It was the highest tribute he could pay to his hero—that he was as faithful as a dog. And think of his services—see him drawing his cart in Belgium, rounding up the sheep into the fold on the Yorkshire fells, tending the cattle by the highway, warning off the night prowler from the lonely homestead, always alert, always obedient, always the friend of man, be he never so friendless.... Shall we go for a walk?

At the joyous word Quilp leapt on me with a frenzied demonstration. "Good dog," I said. "If Mr. McKenna puts a guinea tax on you I'll never say a good word for him again."

"W.G."

The worst of spending week-ends in the country in these anxious days is the difficulty of getting news. About six o'clock on Saturday evening I am seized with a furious hunger. What has happened on the East front? What on the West? What in Serbia? Has Greece made up its heroic mind? Is Rumania still trembling on the brink? What does the French communiqué say? These and a hundred other questions descend on me with frightful insistence. Clearly I can't go to bed without having them answered. But there is not an evening paper to be got nearer than the little railway station in the valley two miles away, and there is no way of getting it except by Shanks' mare. And so, unable to resist the glamour of *The Star*, I start out across the fields for the station.

As I stood on the platform last Saturday evening devouring the latest war news under the dim oil lamp, a voice behind me said, in broad rural accent, "Bill, I say, W.G. is dead." At the word I turned hastily to another column and found the news that had stirred him. And even in the midst of world-shaking events it stirred me too. For a brief moment I forgot the war and was back in that cheerful world where we used to be happy, where we greeted the rising sun with light hearts and saw its setting without fear. In that cheerful world I can hardly recall a time when a big man with a black beard was not my King.

I first saw him in the 'seventies. I was a small boy then, and I did him the honour of playing truant—"playing wag" we called it. I felt that the occasion demanded it. To have the god of my idolatry in my own little town and not to pay him my devotions—why, the idea was almost like blasphemy. A half-dozen, or even a dozen, from my easily infuriated master would be a small price to pay. I should take the stripes as a homage to the hero. He would never know, but I should be proud to suffer in his honour. Unfortunately there was a canvas round the field where the hero played, and as the mark of the Mint was absent from my pockets I was on the wrong side of the canvas. But I knew a spot where by lying flat on your stomach and keeping your head very low you could see under the canvas and get a view of the wicket. It was not a comfortable position, but I saw the King. I think I was a little disappointed that there was nothing supernatural about his appearance and that there were no portents in the heavens to announce his coming. It didn't seem quite right somehow. In a general way I knew he was only a man, but I was quite prepared to see something tremendous happen, the sun to dance or the earth to heave, when he appeared. I never felt the indifference of Nature to the affairs of men so acutely.

I saw him many times afterwards, and I suppose I owe more undiluted happiness to him than to any man that ever lived. For he was the genial tyrant in a world that was all sunshine. There are other games, no doubt, which will give you as much exercise and pleasure in playing them as cricket, but there is no game that fills the mind with such memories and seems enveloped in such a gracious and kindly atmosphere. If you have once loved it and played it, you will find talk in it enough "for the wearing out of six fashions," as Falstaff says. I like a man who has cricket in his soul. I find I am prejudiced in his favour, and am disposed to disbelieve any ill about him. I think my affection for Jorkins began with the discovery that he, like myself, saw that astounding catch with which Ulyett dismissed Bonnor in the Australian match at Lord's in 1883–or was it 1884? And when to this mutual and immortal memory we added the discovery that we were both at the Oval at the memorable match when Crossland rattled Surrey out like ninepins and the crowd mobbed him, and Key and Roller miraculously pulled the game out of the fire, our friendship was sealed.

The fine thing about a wrangle on cricket is that there is no bitterness in it. When you talk about politicians you are always on the brink of bad temper. When you disagree about the relative merits of W.B. Yeats or Francis Thompson you are afflicted with scorn for the other's lack of perception. But you may quarrel about cricketers and love each other all the time. For example, I am prepared to stand up in a truly Christian spirit to the bowling of anybody in defence of my belief that–next to him of the black beard–Lohmann was the most naturally gifted all-round cricketer there has ever been. What grace of action he had, what an instinct for the weak spot of his opponent, what a sense for fitting the action to the moment, above all, what a gallant spirit he played the game in! And that, after all, is the real test of the great cricketer. It is the man who brings the spirit of adventure into the game that I want. Of the Quaifes and the Scottons and the Barlows I have nothing but dreary memories. They do not mean cricket to me. And even Shrewsbury and Hayward left me cold. They were too faultily faultless, too icily regular for my taste. They played cricket not as though it was a game, but as though it was a proposition in Euclid. And I don't like Euclid.

It was the hearty joyousness that "W.G." shed around him that made him so dear to us youngsters of all ages. I will admit, if you like, that Ranjitsinhji at his best was more of a magician with the bat, that Johnny Briggs made you laugh more with his wonderful antics, that A.P. Lucas had more finish, Palairet more grace, and so on. But it was the abundance of the old man with the black beard that was so wonderful. You never came to the end of him. He was like a generous roast of beef–you could cut and come again, and go on coming. Other men flitted across our sky like meteors, but he shone on like the sun in the heavens, and like the sun in the heavens he scattered largesse over the land. He did not seem so much a man as an institution, a symbol of summer and all its joys, a sort of Father Christmas clothed in flannels and sunshine. It did you good merely to look at him. It made you feel happy to see such a huge capacity for enjoyment, such mighty subtlety, such ponderous gaiety. It was as though Jove, or Vulcan, or some other god of antiquity had come down to play games with the mortals. You would not have been much surprised if, when the shadows lengthened across the greensward and the umpire signalled that the day's play was done, he had wrapped himself in a cloud of glory and floated away to Olympus.

And now he is gone indeed, and it seems as though a part, and that a very happy part, of my life has gone with him. When sanity returns to the earth, there will arise other deities of the cricket field, but not for me. Never again shall I recapture the careless rapture that came with the vision of the yellow cap flaming above the black beard, of the Herculean frame and the mighty bared arms, and all the godlike apparition of the master. As I turned out of the little station and passed through the fields and climbed the hill I felt that the darkness that has come upon the earth in these days had taken a deeper shade of gloom, for even the lights of the happy past were being quenched.

ON SEEING VISIONS

The postman (or rather the postwoman) brought me among other things this morning a little paper called *The Superman*, which I find is devoted to the stars, the lines of the hands, and similar mysteries. I gather from it that "Althea," a normal clairvoyant, and other seers, have visited the planets—in their astral bodies, of course—to make inquiries on various aspects of the war. Althea and "the other seers" seem to have had quite a busy time running about among the stars and talking to the inhabitants about the trouble in our particular orb. They seem really to have got to the bottom of things. It appears that there is a row going on between Lucifer and Arniel. "Lucifer is a fallen planetary god, whose lust for power has driven him from his seat of authority as ruler of Jupiter. He is the evil genius overshadowing the Kaiser and is striving to possess this world so that he may pass it on to Jupiter and eventually blot out the Solar Logos," etc., etc.

I do not know who sent me this paper or for what purpose; but let me say that it is sheer waste of postage stamps and material. I hope I am not intolerant of the opinions of others, but I confess that when people talk to me about reading the stars and the lines of the hand and things of that sort I shut up like an oyster. I do not speak of the humbugs who deliberately exploit the credulity of fools. I speak of the sincere believers—people like my dear old friend W.T. Stead, who was the most extraordinary combination of wisdom and moonshine I have ever known. He would startle you at one moment by his penetrating handling of the facts of a great situation, and the next moment would make you speechless with some staggering story of spirit visitors or starry conspiracies that seemed to him just as actual as the pavement on which he walked.

I am not at home in this atmosphere of mysteries. It is not that I do not share the feeling out of which it is born. I do. Thoreau said he would give all he possessed for "one true vision," and so long as we are spiritually alive we must all have some sense of expectancy that the curtain will lift, and that we shall look out with eyes of wonder on the hidden meaning of this strange adventure upon which we are embarked. For thousands of years we have been wandering in this wilderness of the world and speculating about why we are here, where we are going, and what it is all about. It can never have been a greater puzzle than now, when we are all busily engaged in killing each other. And at every stage there have been those who have cried, "Lo, here!" and "Lo, there!" and have called men to witness that they have read the riddle and have torn the secret from the heart of the great mystery.

And so long as men can feel and think, the quest will go on. We could not cease that quest if we would, and we would not if we could, for without it all the meaning would have gone out of life and we should be no more than the cattle in the fields. Nor is the quest in vain. We follow this trail and that, catch at this hint of a meaning and that gleam of vision, and though we find this path ends in a cul-de-sac, and that brings us back to the place from whence we started, we are learning all the time about the mysteries of our wilderness. And one day, perhaps—suddenly, it may be, as that vision of the great white mountains of the Oberland breaks upon the sight of the traveller—we shall see whither the long adventure leads. "Say not the struggle naught availeth," said a poet who was not given to cultivating illusions. And he went on:—

> For while the tired waves, vainly breaking.
> Seem here no painful inch to gain,
> Far back, through creeks and inlets making.
> Comes silent, flooding in, the main.

But though I want to see a vision as much as anybody, I am out of touch with the company of the credulous. I am with Doubting Thomas. I have no capacity for believing the impossible, and have an entire distrust of dark rooms and magic. People with bees in their bonnets leave me wondering, but cold. I know a man—a most excellent man—whose life is a perfect debauch of visions and revelations. He seems to discover the philosopher's stone every other day. Sometimes it is brown bread that is the way to salvation. If you eat brown bread you will never die, or at any rate you will live until everybody is tired of you. Sometimes it is a new tax or a new sort of bath that is the secret key to the whole contraption. For one period he could talk of nothing but dried milk; for another, acetic acid was the thing. Rub yourself with acetic acid and you would be as invulnerable to the ills of the body as Achilles was after he had been dipped by Thetis in the waters of Styx. The stars tell him anything he wishes to believe, and he can conjure up spirits as easily as another man can order a cab. It is not that he is a fool. In practical affairs he is astonishingly astute. It is that he has an illimitable capacity for belief. He is always on the road to Damascus.

For my part I am content to wait. I am for Wordsworth's creed of "wise passiveness." I should as soon think of reading my destiny on the sole of my boot as in the palm of my hand. The one would be just as illuminating as the other. It would tell me what I chose to make it tell me. That and no more. And so with the stars. People who pretend to read the riddle of our affairs in the pageant of the stars are deceiving themselves or are trying to deceive others. They are giving their own little fancies the sanction of the universe. The butterfly that I see flitting about in the sunshine outside might as well read the European war as a comment on its aimless little life. The stars do not chatter about us, but they have a balm for us if we will be silent. The "huge and thoughtful night" speaks a language simple, august, universal.

It is one of the smaller consolations of the war that it has given us in London a chance of hearing that language. The lamps of the street are blotted out, and the lamps above are visible. Five nights of the week all the year round I take the last bus that goes northward from the City, and from the back seat on the top I watch the great procession of the stars. It is the most astonishing spectacle offered to men. Emerson said that if we only saw it once in a hundred years we should spend years in preparing for the vision. It is hung out for us every night, and we hardly give it a glance. And yet it is well worth glancing at. It is the best corrective for this agitated little mad-house in which we dwell and quarrel and fight and die. It gives us a new scale of measurement and a new order of ideas. Even the war seems only a local affair of some ill-governed asylum in the presence of this ordered march of illimitable worlds. I do not worry about the vision; I do not badger the stars to give me their views about the war. It is enough to see and feel and be silent.

And now I hope Althea will waste no more postage stamps in sending me her desecrating gibberish.

ON BLACK SHEEP

When I was in France a few weeks ago I heard much about the relative qualities of different classes of men as soldiers. And one of the most frequent themes was the excellence of the "black sheep." It was not merely that he was brave. That one might expect. It was not even that he was unselfish. That also did not arouse surprise. The pride in him, I found, was chiefly due to the fact that he was so good a soldier in the sense of discipline, enthusiasm, keenness, even intelligence. It is, I believe, a well-ascertained fact that an unusually high proportion of reformatory boys and other socially doubtful men have won rewards for exceptional deeds, and everyone knows the case of the man with twenty-seven convictions against him who won the V.C. for one of the bravest acts of the war.

It must not be assumed from this that to be a successful soldier you must be a social failure. On the contrary, nothing has been so conclusively proved by this war as the widespread prevalence of the soldierly instinct. Heroes have sprung up from all ranks and all callings—from drapers' shops and furniture vans, from stools in the city and looms in Lancashire, from Durham pits and bishops' palaces. Whatever else the war has done, it has knocked on the head the idea that the cult of militarism is necessary to preserve the soul of courage and chivalry in a people. We, with a wholly civic tradition, have shown that in the hour of need we can draw upon an infinite reservoir of heroism, as splendid as anything in the annals of the human race.

But the case of the black sheep has a special significance for us. The war has discovered the good that is in him, and has released it for useful service. After all, the black sheep is often only black by the accident of circumstance, upbringing, or association. He is a misfit. In him, as in all of us, there is an infinite complexity—good and ill together. No one who has faithfully examined his own life can doubt how trifling a weight turns the scales for or against us. An accidental meeting, a casual friendship, a phrase in a book—and the current of life takes a definite direction this way or that. There are no doubt people in whom the elements are so perfectly adjusted that the balance is never in doubt. Their character is superior to circumstance. But they are rare. They are the stars that dwell apart from our human struggles. Most of us know what it is to be on the brink of the precipice—know, if we are quite honest with ourselves, how narrow a shave we have had from joining the black sheep. Perhaps, if we are still honest with ourselves, we shall admit that the thing that turned the balance for us was not a very creditable thing—that we were protected from ourselves not by any high virtue, but by something mean, a touch of cowardice, a paltry ambition, a consideration that we should be ashamed to confess.

We are so strangely compact that we do not ourselves know what the ordeal will discover in us. You have no doubt read that incident of the sergeant who, in a moment of panic, fled, was placed under arrest and sentenced to be shot. Before the sentence was ratified by the Commander-in-Chief, there came a moment of extreme peril to the line, when irretrievable disaster was imminent and every man who could fill a gap was needed. The condemned man was called out to face the enemy, and, even in the midst of brave men, fought with a bravery that singled him out for the Victoria Cross. Tell me— which was the true man? I saw the other day a letter from a famous doctor dealing with the question of the psychology of war. He was against shooting a man for cowardice, because cowardice was not necessarily a quality of character. It was often a temporary collapse due to physical fatigue, or a passing condition of mind. "Five times," he said, "I have been at work in circumstances in which my life was in imminent peril. On four occasions I worked with a curious sense of exaltation. On the fifth occasion I was seized with a sudden and unreasoning panic that paralysed me. Perhaps it was a failure of digestion, perhaps a want of sleep. Anyhow, at that moment I was a coward."

The truth is that, except for the aforesaid stars who dwell apart, we all have the potential saint and the potential sinner, the hero and the coward, the honest man and the dishonest man within us.

There is a fine poem in *A Shropshire Lad* that puts the case of the black sheep as pregnantly as it can be put:—

There sleeps in Shrewsbury gaol to-night,
Or wakes, as may betide,
A better lad if things went right
Than most that sleep outside.

If things went right.... Do not, I pray you, think that in saying this I am holding the candle to that deadly doctrine of determinism, or that, like the tragic novelist, I see man only as a pitiful animal caught in the trap of blind circumstance. If I believed that I should say "Better dead." But what I do say is that we are so variously composed that circumstance does play a powerful part in giving rein to this or that element in us and making the scale go down for good or bad, and that often the best of us only miss the wrong turning by a hair's breadth. Dirt, it is said, is only matter in the wrong place. Put it in the right place, and it ceases to be dirt. Give that man with twenty-seven convictions against him a chance of revealing the better metal that is in him, and, lo! he is hailed as a hero and decorated with the V.C.

THE VILLAGE AND THE WAR

"Well, have you heard the news?"

It was the landlord of the Blue Boar who spoke. He stopped me in the village street—if you can call a straggling lane with a score of thatched cottages and half a dozen barns a street—evidently bursting with great tidings. He is an old soldier himself, and his views on the war are held in great esteem. I hadn't heard the news, but, whatever it was, I could see from the landlord's immense smile that there was nothing to fear.

"Jim has got a commission," said the landlord, and he said it in a tone that left no doubt that now things would begin to move. For Jim is his son, a sergeant-major in the artillery, who has been out at the front ever since Mons.

The news has created quite a sensation. But we are getting so used to sensations now that we are becoming *blasé*. There has never been such a year of wonders in the memory of anyone living. The other day thousands of soldiers from the great camp ten miles away descended on our "terrain"—I think that's the word—and had a tremendous two-days' battle in the hills about us. They broke through the hedges, and slept in the cornfields, and ravished the apple-trees in my orchard, and raided the cottagers for tea, and tramped to and fro in our street and gave us the time of our lives.

"*I* never seed such a sight in *my* life," said old Benjamin to me in the evening. "Man and boy, I've lived in that there bungalow for eighty-five year come Michaelmas, and *I* never seed the like o' *this* before.... Yes, eighty-five year come Michaelmas. And my father had that there land on a peppercorn rent, and the way he lost it was like this—"

Happily at this moment there was a sudden alarum among the soldiers, and I was able to dodge the familiar rehearsal of old Benjamin's grievance.

And who would ever have dreamed that we should live to hear French talked in our street as a familiar form of speech? But we have. In a little cottage at the other end of the village is a family of Belgians, a fragment of the flotsam thrown up by the great inundation of 1914. They have brought the story of "frightfulness" near to us, for they passed through the terror of Louvain, hiding in the cellars for nights and days, having two of their children killed, and escaping to the coast on foot.

Every Sunday night you will see them very busy carrying their few chairs and tables into a neighbouring barn, for on Monday mornings mass is celebrated there. The priest comes up in a country cart from ten miles away, and the refugees scattered for miles around assemble for worship, after which there is a tremendous pow-pow in French and Flemish, with much laughter and gaiety.

Old Benjamin "don't hold with they priests," and he has grave suspicions about all foreign tongues, but the Belgians have become quite a part of us, and their children are learning to lisp in English down at the school in the valley.

Much less agreeable is the frame of mind towards the occupants of the cottage next to the Blue Boar. They are the wife and children of a German who had worked in this country for many years and is now in America. The woman is English and amiable, but the proximity of anything so reminiscent of Germany is painful to the village, and especially to the landlord, whose views about Germans can hardly be put into words.

"I should hope there'll be no prisoners took after *this*," he says grimly whenever he hears of a new outrage. "Vermin—that's what they are," he says, "and they should be treated according-ly."

The Germans, in fact, have become the substitute for every term of execration, even with mild David the labourer. He came into the orchard last evening staggering under a 15-ft. ladder. We had decided that if we were going to have the pears before the wasps had spoiled them we must pick them at once.

"It's a wunnerful crop," said David. "I've knowed this pear-tree [looking up at one of them from the foot of his ladder] for twenty-five year, and I've never seen such a crop on it afore."

Then he mounted the ladder and began to pick the fruit.

"Well, I'm blowed," he said, "if they ain't been at 'em a'ready." And he flung down pear after pear scooped out by the wasps close to the stalk. "Reg'lar Germans—that's what they are," he said. "Look at 'em round that hive," he went on. "They'll hev all the honey and them bees will starve and git the Isle o' Wight—that's what they'll git.... Lor," he added, reflectively, "I dunno what wospses are made for—wospses *and* Germans. It gits over me."

I said it got over me too. And then from among the branches, while I hung on to the foot of the ladder to keep it firm, David unbosomed his disquiet to me about enlisting.

"Most o' the chaps round here has gone," he said, "an' I don't like staying be'ind. Seems as though you were hanging back like. 'Taint that I shouldn't like to go; but it's this way ... (Hullo, I got my hand on a wasp that time) ... There's such a lot o' women-folk dependent on me. There's my wife and there's my mother down the village *and* my aunt; and not a man to do anything for 'em but me. After my work on th' farm, I keeps all three gardens going and a patch of allotment down the valley as well."

"You're growing a lot of good food, and that's military work," I said.

He seemed cheered by the idea, and asked me if I'd like to see the potatoes he had dug up that evening—they were "a wunnerful fine lot," he said.

So after he had stripped the pear-tree he shouldered the ladder, and we went down the village to David's garden. There I saw his potatoes, some lying to dry where they had been dug up, others in sacks. Also his marrows and beans and cabbages and lettuces. A little apologetically, he offered me some of the largest potatoes—"just as a hobby," he said, meaning thereby that it was only a trifle he offered.

As I went away in the gathering dark, with my hands full of potatoes, I met the landlord of the Blue Boar, his shirt sleeves rolled up as usual above his brown, muscular arms.

"Bad news that about Mrs. Lummis," he said, looking towards the cottage on the other side of the road.

"What is that?" said I. "Her son?" There had been no news of him for two months.

"Yes, poor Jack. She's got news that he was killed near la Bassée in June. Nice feller—and her only son."

Then, more cheerfully, he added, "Jim's coming home to-morrow. Going to get his officer's rig out, you know, and have a rest—the first since he went out a year ago."

"You'll be glad to see him," said I.

"Not half," said he with a vast smile.

ON RUMOUR

I was speaking the other day to a man of cautious mind on a subject of current rumour. "Well," he said, "if I had been asked whether I believed such evidence four months ago I should have said 'Certainly.' But after the great Russian myth I believe nothing that I can't prove. I believed in that army of ghosts that came from Archangel! There are people who say they didn't believe in it. Some of them believe they didn't believe in it. But I say defiantly that I did believe in it. And I say further that there was never a rumour in the world that seemed based upon more various or more convincing evidence. And it wasn't true.... Well, I find I'm a changed man. I find I am no longer a believer: I am a doubter."

This experience, I suppose, is not uncommon. The man who believes as easily to-day as he did six months ago is a man on whom lessons are thrown away. We have lived in a world of gigantic whispers, and most of them have been false whispers. Even the magic word "Official" leaves one cold. It is not what I am "officially" told that interests me: it is what I am "officially" not told that I want to know in order to arrive at the truth.

You remember that famous answer of the plaintiff in an action against a London paper years ago. "What did you tell him?" "I told him to tell the truth." "The whole truth?" "No, *selected truths.*"

What we have to guard against in this matter of rumours is the natural tendency to believe what we want to believe. Take that case of the reported victory in Poland in November 1914. There is strong reason to believe that a large part of Hindenburg's army narrowly escaped being encircled, that had Rennenkampf come up to time the trick would have been done. But it wasn't done. Yet nearly every correspondent in Petrograd sent the most confident news of an overwhelming victory. The *Morning Post* correspondent spoke of it as something "terrible but sublime. There has been nothing like it since Napoleon left the bones of half a million men behind him in Russia." Even Lord Kitchener, in the House of Lords, said that Russia had accomplished the greatest achievement of the war. And so, just afterwards, with the equally empty rumour of Hindenburg's "victory," which sent Berlin into such a frenzy of rejoicing. It believed without evidence because it wanted to believe.

And another fruitful source of rumour is fear. The famous concrete emplacement at Maubeuge will serve as an instance. We had the most elaborate details of how the property was acquired by German agents, how in secret the concrete platform was laid down, and how the great 42-cm. howitzer shelled Maubeuge from it. And instantly we heard of concrete emplacements in this country—at Willesden, Edinburgh, and elsewhere. We began to suspect everyone who had a garage or a machine shop with a concrete foundation of being a German agent. I confess that I shared these suspicions in regard to a certain factory overlooking London, and could not wholly argue myself out of them, though I hadn't an atom of evidence beyond the fact that the building had been owned by Germans and had a commanding position. I was under the hypnotism of Maubeuge and the fears to which it gave birth.

Yet there never was a concrete emplacement at Maubeuge, and no 42-cm. howitzer was used against that fortress. The property belonged, not to German agents, but to respectable Frenchmen, and the apology of the *Matin* for the libel upon them may be read by anybody who is interested in these myths of the war.

I refer to this subject to-day not to recall these historic fables, but to show what cruel wrong we may do to the innocent by accepting rumours about our neighbours without examining the facts. Was there ever a more pitiful story than that told at the inquest on an elderly woman at Henham in Suffolk? Her husband had been the village schoolmaster for twenty-eight years. The couple had a son whom they sent to Germany to learn the language. The average village schoolmaster has not much money for luxuries, and I can imagine the couple screwing and saving to give their boy a good start in life. When he had finished his training he set out to seek his fortune in South America, and there in far Guatemala he became a teacher of languages. When the war broke out he heard the call of the Motherland to her children and like thousands of others came back to fight.

But in the meantime the lying tongue of rumour had been busy with his name in his native village. It was said that he was an officer in the German Army, and on the strength of that rumour his parents were ordered by the Chief Constable to leave the village and not to dwell on the East Coast. It was a sentence of death on them. The order broke the old man's heart, and he committed suicide. The son arrived to find his father dead and his mother distracted by her bereavement. He took her away to the seaside for a rest, but on their return to the village she, too, committed suicide. And the jury did not say "Killed by Slander": they said "Suicide while of unsound mind." Oh, cautious jurymen!

How do rumours get abroad? There are many ways. Let me illustrate one of them. In his criticism of the war the other week Mr. Belloc said:

"The official German communiqué which appeared in print last Saturday is a very good example upon which to work. I quote it as it appeared in the *Westminster Gazette* (*which has from the beginning of the war, and even before its outbreak, been remarkable for the volume of its German information*), and as it was delivered through the Marconi channel."

Then follows the communiqué. Now, when I read this I smiled, for I love the subtleties of the ingenious Mr. Belloc. He quotes a document which appeared in every paper in the country, but he says he quotes it from the *Westminster Gazette*. Why, since it appeared everywhere, does he mention one paper? Obviously in order to make that parenthetical remark which I have italicised.

Now the reputation of the *Westminster* stands too high to be affected by the suggestion that it is "remarkable"–which it isn't–for its German information. But suppose you, a mere ordinary citizen, were alleged by someone to have special intercourse with Germany at this time. You might be as innocent as that Suffolk schoolmaster, but that would not save you from the suspicions of your neighbours and, perhaps, the attentions of the Chief Constable.

Let me give another little illustration. A friend of mine, who happens to be a Liberal journalist, went to a private dinner recently to meet M. Painlevé, the French Academician, Senator Lafontaine, of Brussels, and two other French and Belgian deputies. The next morning he was stated in the *Daily Express* (edited by Mr. Blumenfeld) to have dined with "*three or four foreigners*" for the purpose of discussing peace. And in the next issue of the *London Mail* the question was asked, "Who were the foreigners with whom —— dined?" You see the insinuation. You see how the idea grows. He did not reply, because there are some papers that one can afford to ignore, no matter what they say. But I mention the thing here to show how a legend is launched.

And the moral of all this? It is that of my friend whom I have quoted. Let us suspect all rumours whether about events or persons. When Napoleon's marshals told him they had won a victory, he said, "Show me your prisoners." When you are told a rumour do not swallow it like a hungry pike. Say "Show me your facts." And before you accept them be sure they are whole facts and not half facts.

ON UMBRELLA MORALS

A sharp shower came on as I walked along the Strand, but I did not put up my umbrella. The truth is I couldn't put up my umbrella. The frame would not work for one thing, and if it had worked, I would not have put the thing up, for I would no more be seen under such a travesty of an umbrella than Falstaff would be seen marching through Coventry with his regiment of ragamuffins. The fact is, the umbrella is not my umbrella at all. It is the umbrella of some person who I hope will read these lines. He has got my silk umbrella. I have got the cotton one he left in exchange. I imagine him flaunting along the Strand under my umbrella, and throwing a scornful glance at the fellow who was carrying his abomination and getting wet into the bargain. I daresay the rascal chuckled as he eyed the said abomination. "Ah," he said gaily to himself, "I did you in that time, old boy. I know that thing. It won't open for nuts. And it folds up like a sack. Now, this umbrella...."

But I leave him to his unrighteous communings. He is one of those people who have what I may call an umbrella conscience. You know the sort of person I mean. He would never put his hand in another's pocket, or forge a cheque or rob a till—not even if he had the chance. But he will swop umbrellas, or forget to return a book, or take a rise out of the railway company. In fact he is a thoroughly honest man who allows his honesty the benefit of the doubt. Perhaps he takes your umbrella at random from the barber's stand. He knows he can't get a worse one than his own. He may get a better. He doesn't look at it very closely until he is well on his way. Then, "Dear me! I've taken the wrong umbrella," he says, with an air of surprise, for he likes really to feel that he has made a mistake. "Ah, well, it's no use going back now. He'd be gone. *And I've left him mine!*"

It is thus that we play hide-and-seek with our own conscience. It is not enough not to be found out by others; we refuse to be found out by ourselves. Quite impeccable people, people who ordinarily seem unspotted from the world, are afflicted with umbrella morals. It was a well-known preacher who was found dead in a first-class railway carriage with a third-class ticket in his pocket.

And as for books, who has any morals where they are concerned? I remember some years ago the library of a famous divine and literary critic, who had died, being sold. It was a splendid library of rare books, chiefly concerned with seventeenth-century writers, about whom he was a distinguished authority. Multitudes of the books had the marks of libraries all over the country. He had borrowed them and never found a convenient opportunity of returning them. They clung to him like precedents to law. Yet he was a holy man and preached admirable sermons, as I can bear witness. And, if you press me on the point, I shall have to own that it *is* hard to part with a book you have come to love.

Indeed, the only sound rule about books is that adopted by the man who was asked by a friend to lend him a certain volume. "I'm sorry," he said, "but I can't." "Haven't you got it?" asked the other. "Yes, I've got it," he said, "but I make it a rule never to lend books. You see, nobody ever returns them. I know it is so from my own experience. Here, come with me." And he led the way to his library. "There," said he, "four thousand volumes. Every—one—of—'em—borrowed." No, never lend books. You can't trust your dearest friend there. I know. Where is that *Gil Blas* gone? Eh? And that *Silvio Pellico*? And.... But why continue the list.... He knows. HE KNOWS.

And hats. There are people who will exchange hats. Now that is unpardonable. That goes outside that dim borderland of conscience where honesty and dishonesty dissemble. No one can put a strange hat on without being aware of the fact. Yet it is done. I once hung a silk hat up in the smoking-room of the House of Commons. When I wanted it, it was gone. And there was no silk hat left in its place. I had to go out bareheaded through Palace Yard and Whitehall to buy another. I have often wondered who was the gentleman who put my hat on and carried his own in his hand. Was he a Tory? Was he a Radical? It can't have been a Labour man, for no Labour man could put a silk hat on in a moment of abstraction. The thing would scorch his brow. Fancy Will Crooks in a silk hat! One would as soon dare to play with the fancy of the Archbishop of Canterbury in a bowler—a thought which seems almost impious. It is possible, of course, that the gentleman who took my silk umbrella did really make a mistake. Perhaps if he knew the owner he would return it with his compliments. The thing has been done. Let me give an illustration. I have myself exchanged umbrellas—often. I hope I have done it honestly, but one can never be quite sure. Indeed, now I come to think of it, that silk umbrella itself was not mine. It was one of a long series of exchanges in which I had sometimes gained and sometimes lost. My most memorable exchange was at a rich man's house where I had been invited to dine with some politicians. It was summer-time, and the weather being dry I had not occasion for some days afterwards to carry an umbrella. Then one day a sensation reigned in our household. There had been discovered in the umbrella-stand an umbrella with a gold band and a gold tassle, and the name of a certain statesman engraved upon it. There had never been such a super-umbrella in our house before. Before its golden splendours we were at once humbled and terrified—humbled by its magnificence, terrified by its presence. I felt as though I had been caught in the act of stealing the British Empire. I wrote a hasty letter to the owner, told him I admired his politics, but had never hoped to steal his umbrella; then hailed a cab, and took the umbrella and the note to the nearest dispatch office.

He was very nice about it, and in returning my own umbrella took all the blame on himself. "What," he said, "between the noble-looking gentleman who thrust a hat on my head, and the second noble-looking gentleman who handed me a coat, and the third noble-looking gentleman who put an umbrella in my hand, and the fourth noble-looking gentleman who flung me into a carriage, I hadn't the least idea what I was taking. I was too bewildered by all the noble flunkeys to refuse anything that was offered me."

Be it observed, it was the name on the umbrella that saved the situation in this case. That is the way to circumvent the man with an umbrella conscience. I see him eyeing his exchange with a secret joy; then he observes the name and address and his solemn conviction that he is an honest man does the rest. After my experience to-day, I think I will engrave my name on my umbrella. But not on that baggy thing standing in the corner. I do not care who relieves me of that. It is anybody's for the taking.

ON TALKING TO ONE'S SELF

I was at dinner at a well-known restaurant the other evening when I became aware that someone sitting alone at a table nearby was engaged in an exciting conversation with himself. As he bent over his plate his face was contorted with emotion, apparently intense anger, and he talked with furious energy, only pausing briefly in the intervals of actual mastication. Many glances were turned covertly upon him, but he seemed wholly unconscious of them, and, so far as I could judge, he was unaware that he was doing anything abnormal. In repose his face was that of an ordinary business man, sane and self-controlled, and when he rose to go his agitation was over, and he looked like a man who had won his point.

It is probable that this habit of talking to one's self has a less sinister meaning than it superficially suggests. It may be due simply to the energy of one's thought and to a concentration of mind that completely shuts out the external world. In the case I have mentioned it was clear that the man was temporarily detached from all his surroundings, that he was so absorbed by his subject that his eyes had ceased to see and his ears to hear. He was alone with himself, or perhaps with his adversary, and he only came back to the present with the end of his dinner and the paying of his bill. He was like a man who had emerged from another state of consciousness, from a waking sleep filled with tumultuous dreams. Obviously he was unaware that he had been haranguing the room in quite an audible voice for half an hour, and I daresay that if he were told that he had the habit of talking to himself he would deny it as passionately as you (or I) would deny that you (or I) snore in our sleep. And he would deny it for precisely the same reason. He doesn't know.

And here a dreadful thought assails me. What if I talk to myself, too? What if, like this man, I get so absorbed in the drama of my own mind that I cannot hear my own tongue going nineteen to the dozen? It is a disquieting idea. A strong conviction to the contrary, I see, amounts to nothing. This man, doubtless, had a strong conviction to the contrary—probably expressed an amused interest in any one talking to himself as he passed him in the street. And the fact that my friends have never told me of the failing goes for nothing also. They may think I like to talk to myself. More probably, they may know that I do not like to hear of my failings. I must watch myself. But, no, that won't do. I might as well say I would watch my dreams and keep them in check. How can the conscious state keep an eye on the unconscious? If I do not know that I am talking how can I stop myself talking?

Ah, happy thought. I recall occasions when I have talked to myself, and have been quite conscious of the sound of my voice. They have been remarks I have made on the golf links, brief, emphatic remarks dealing with the perversity of golf clubs and the sullen intractability of golf balls. Those remarks I have heard distinctly, and at the sound of them I have come to myself with a shock, and have even looked round to see whether the lady in the red jacket playing at the next hole was likely to have heard me or (still worse) to have seen me.

I think this is evidence conclusive, for the man who talks to himself habitually never hears himself. His words are only the echo of his thoughts, and they correspond so perfectly that, like a chord in music, there is no dissonance. It was thus with the art student I saw copying a picture at the Tate Gallery. "Ah, a little more blue," he said, as he turned from the original to his own canvas, and a little later: "Yes, that line wants better drawing." Several people stood by watching his work and smiling at his uttered thoughts. He alone was unconscious that he had spoken.

There are, it is true, cases in which the conscious and unconscious states seem to mingle–in which the intentional word and the unintentional come out almost in the same breath. It was so with Thomas Landseer, the father of Sir Edwin. He was one day visiting an artist, and inspecting his work. "Ah, very nice, indeed!" he said to his friend. "Excellent colour; excellent!" Then, as if all around him had vanished, and he was alone with himself, he added: "Poor chap, he thinks he can paint!"

And this instance shows that whether the habit is a mental weakness or only a physical defect it is capable of extremely awkward consequences, as in the case of the banker who was ruined by unwittingly revealing his secrets while walking in the street. How is it possible to keep a secret or conduct a bargain if your tongue is uncontrollable? What is the use of Jones explaining to his wife that he has been kept late at the office if his tongue goes on to say, entirely without his knowledge or consent, that had he declared "no trumps" in that last hand he would have been in pocket by his evening at the club? I see horrible visions of domestic complications and public disaster arising from this not uncommon habit.

And yet might there not be gain also from a universal practice of uttering our thoughts aloud? Imagine a world in which nobody had any secrets from anybody–could have no secrets from anybody. I see the Kaiser, after consciously declaring that his only purpose is peace, unconsciously blurting out to the British Ambassador that the ultimatum to Serbia is a "plant"–that what Germany means is war, that she proposes to attack Belgium, and so on. And I see the British Ambassador, having explained that England is entirely free from commitments, adding dreamily, "But if there's a war we shall be in it." In the same way Jones, after making Smith a firm offer of £30 for his horse, would say, absentmindedly, "Of course it would be cheap at £50, and I might spring £55 if he is stiff about it."

It would be a world in which lies would have no value and deception would be a waste of time–a world in which truth would no longer be at the bottom of the well, but on the tip of every man's tongue. We should have all the rascals in prison and all the dishonest traders in the bankruptcy court. Secret diplomacy would no longer play with the lives of men, for there would be no secrets. Those little perverse concealments that wreck so many lives would vanish. You, sir, who find it so easy to nag at home and so difficult to say the kind thing that you know to be true, would be discovered to your great advantage and to the peace of your household.

Yes, I think the world would go very well if we all had tongues that told our true thoughts in spite of us. But what a lot of us would be found out. My own face crimsons at the thought. So, I think, does yours.

ON BOSWELL AND HIS MIRACLE

As I passed along Great Queen Street the other evening, I saw that Boswell's house, so long threatened, is at last falling a victim to the housebreaker. The fact is one of the by-products of the war. While the Huns are abroad in Belgium the Vandals are busy at home. You may see them at work on every hand. The few precious remains we have of the past are vanishing like snows before the south wind.

In the Strand there is a great heap of rubbish where, when the war began, stood two fine old houses of Charles II.'s London. Their disappearance would, in normal times, have set all the Press in revolt. But they have gone without a murmur, so preoccupied are we with more urgent matters. And so with the Elizabethan houses in Cloth Fair. They have been demolished without a word of protest. And what devastation is afoot in Lincoln's Inn among those fine reposeful dwellings, hardly one of which is without some historic or literary interest!

In the midst of all this vandalism it was too much perhaps to hope that Boswell's house would escape. Bozzy was not an Englishman; his residence in London was casual, and, what is more to the point, he has only a reflected greatness. Macaulay's judgment of him is now felt to be too harsh, but even his warmest advocate must admit that his picture of himself is not engaging. He was gross in his habits, full of little malevolences (observe the spitefulness of his references to Goldsmith), and his worship of Johnson was abject to the point of nausea.

He made himself a sort of doormat for his hero, and treasured the dirt that came from the great man's heavy boots. No insult levelled at him was too outrageous to be recorded with pride. "You were drunk last night, you dog," says Johnson to him one morning during the tour in the Hebrides, and down goes the remark as if he has received the most gracious of good mornings. "Have you no better manners?" says Johnson on another occasion. "There is *your want*." And Boswell goes home and writes down the snub together with his apologies. And so when he has been expressing his emotions on hearing music. "Sir," said Johnson, "I should never hear it if it made me such a fool."

Once indeed he rebelled. It was when they were dining with a company at Sir Joshua Reynolds's. Johnson attacked him, he says, with such rudeness that he kept away from him for a week. His story of the reconciliation is one of the most delightful things in that astonishing book:

"After dinner, when Mr. Langton was called out of the room and we were by ourselves, he drew his chair near to mine and said, in a tone of conciliatory courtesy, 'Well, how have you done?' Boswell: 'Sir, you have made me very uneasy by your behaviour to me when we were last at Sir Joshua Reynolds's. You know, my dear sir, no man has a greater respect or affection for you, or would sooner go to the end of the world to serve you. Now, to treat me so—' He insisted that I had interrupted him, which

I assured him was not the case; and proceeded, 'But why treat me so before people who neither love you nor me?' Johnson: 'Well I am sorry for it. I'll make it up to you in twenty different ways, as you please.' Boswell: 'I said to-day to Sir Joshua, when he observed that you *tossed* me sometimes, I don't care how often or how high he tosses me when only friends are present, for then I fall upon soft ground; but I do not like falling upon stones, which is the case when enemies are present. I think this is a pretty good image, sir.' Johnson: 'Sir, it is one of the happiest I ever have heard.'"

Is there anything more delicious outside Falstaff and Bardolph, or Don Quixote and Sancho Panza? Indeed, Bardolph's immortal "Would I were with him wheresoe'er he be, whether in heaven or in hell," is in the very spirit of Boswell's devotion to his hero.

It was his failings as much as his talents that enabled him to work the miracle. His lack of self-respect and humour, his childish egotism, his love of gossip, his naive bathos, and his vulgarities contributed as much to the making of his immortal book as his industry, his wonderful verbal memory, and his doglike fidelity. I have said that his greatness is only reflected. But that is hardly just. It might even be more true to say that Johnson owes his immortality to Boswell. What of him would remain to-day but for the man who took his scourgings so humbly and repaid them by licking the boot that kicked him? Who now reads *London,* or *The Vanity of Human Wishes,* or *The Rambler*? I once read *Rasselas,* and found it pompous and dull. And I have read *The Lives of the Poets,* and though they are not pompous and dull, they are often singularly poor criticism, and the essay on Milton is, in some respects, as mean a piece of work as ever came out of Grub Street.

But *The Life*! What in all the world of books is there like it? I have been reading it off and on for more than thirty years, and still find it inexhaustible. It ripens with the years. It is so intimate that it seems to be a record of my own experiences. I have dined so often with Johnson at the Mitre and Sir Joshua's and Langton's and the rest that I know him far better than the shadows I meet in daily life. I seem to have been present when he was talking to the King, and when Goldsmith sulked because he had not shared the honour; when he met Wilkes, and when he insulted Sir Joshua and for once got silenced; when he "downed" Robertson, and when, for want of a lodging, he and Savage walked all night round St. James's Square, full of high spirits and patriotism, inveighing against the Minister and resolving that "they would *stand by their country*."

And at the end of it all I feel very much like Mr. Birrell, who, when asked what he would do when the Government went out of office, replied, "I shall retire to the country, and really read Boswell." Not "finish Boswell," you observe. No one could ever finish Boswell. No one would ever want to finish Boswell. Like a sensible man he will just go on reading him and reading him, and reading him until the light fails and there is no more reading to be done.

What an achievement for this uncouth Scotch lawyer to have accomplished! He knew he had done a great thing; but even he did not know how great a thing. Had he known he might have answered as proudly as Dryden answered when someone said to him that his *Ode to St. Cecilia* was the finest that had ever been written. "Or ever will be," said the poet. Dryden's ode has been eclipsed more than once since it was written; but Boswell's book has never been approached. It is not only the best thing of its sort in literature: there is nothing with which one can compare it.

Boswell's house is falling to dust. No matter! His memorial will last as long as the English speech is spoken and as long as men love the immortal things of which it is the vehicle.

ON SEEING OURSELVES

A friend of mine who is intimate enough with me to guess my secrets, said to me quizzingly the other day: "Do you know 'Alpha of the Plough?'"

"I have never seen the man," I said promptly and unblushingly. He laughed and I laughed.

"What, never?" he said.

"Never," I said. "What's more, I never shall see him."

"What, not in the looking-glass?" said he.

"That's not 'Alpha of the Plough,'" I answered. "That is only his counterfeit. It may be a good counterfeit, but it's not the man. The man I shall never see. I can see bits of him—his hands, his feet, his arms, and so on. By shutting one eye I can see something of the shape of his nose. By thrusting out the upper lip I can see that the fellow wears a moustache. But his face, as a whole, is hidden from me. I cannot tell you even with the help of the counterfeit what impression he makes on the beholder. Now," I continued, pausing and taking stock of my friend, "I know what you are like. I take you all in at one glance. You can take me in at a glance. The only person we can none of us take in at a glance is the person we should most like to see."

"It's a mercy," said he.

I am not sure that he was right. In this matter, as in most things in this perplexing world, there is much to be said on both sides. It is lucky for some of us undoubtedly that we are condemned to be eternal strangers to ourselves, and that not merely to our physical selves. We do not know even the sound of our own voices. Mr. Pemberton-Billing has never heard the most sepulchral voice in the House of Commons, and Lord Charles Beresford does not know how a foghorn sounds when it becomes articulate. I have no idea, and you have no idea, what sort of impression our manner makes on others. If we had, how stricken some of us would be! We should hardly survive the revelation. We should be sorry we had ever been born.

Imagine, for example, that eminent politician, Mr. Sutherland Bangs, M.P., meeting himself out at a dinner one evening. Mr. Sutherland Bangs cherishes a comfortable vision of himself as a handsome, engaging fellow, with a gift for talk, a breezy manner, a stylish presence, and an elegant accent. And seated beside himself at dinner he would discover that he was a pretentious bore, that his talk was windy commonplace, his breezy manner an offence, his fine accent an unpleasant affectation. He would say that he would never want to see that fellow again. And, realising that that was Mr. Sutherland Bangs as he appears to the world, he would return home as humble and abject as Mr. Tom Lofty in *The Good-Natured Man* was when his imposture was found out. "You ought to have your head stuck in a pillory," said Mr. Croaker. "Stick it where you will," said Mr. Lofty, "for by the lord, it cuts a poor figure where it sticks at present." Mr. Sutherland Bangs would feel like that.

But if making our own acquaintance would give some of us a good deal of surprise and even pain, it would also do most of us a useful turn as well. Burns put the case quite clearly in his familiar lines:

> O wad some pow'r the giftie gie us
> To see oursels as others see us:
> It wad frae monie a blunder free us
> An' foolish notion.

We should all make discoveries to our advantage as well as our discomfiture. You, sir, might find that the talent for argument on which you pride yourself is to me only irritating wrong-headedness, and I might find that the bright wit that I fancy I flash around makes you feel tired. Jones's eyeglass would drop out of his eye because he would know it only made him look foolish, Brown would see the ugliness of his cant, and Robinson would sorry that he had been born a bully and as prickly as a hedgehog. It would do us all good to get this objective view of ourselves.

It is not necessarily the right view or the complete view. You remember that ingenious fancy of Holmes' about John and Thomas. They are talking together and don't quite hit it off, and Holmes says it is no wonder since six persons are engaged in the conversation. "Six!" you say, lifting your eyebrows. Yes, six, says he. There is John's ideal John—that is, John as he appears to himself; Thomas's ideal John—that is, John as Thomas sees him; and the real John, known only to his Maker. And so with Thomas, there are three of him engaged in the talk also. Now John's ideal John is not a bit like Thomas's ideal John, and neither of them is like the real John, and so it comes about that John and Thomas—that is, you and I—get at cross purposes.

If I (John) could have your (Thomas's) glimpse of myself, my appearance, my manner, my conduct, and so on, it would serve as a valuable corrective. It would give that faculty of self-criticism which most of us lack. That faculty is simply the art of seeing ourselves objectively, as a stranger sees us who has no interest in us and no prejudice in our favour. Few of us can do that except in fleeting flashes of illumination. We cannot even do it in regard to the things we produce. If you paint a picture, or write an article, or make a joke, you are pretty sure to be a bad judge of its quality. You only see it subjectively as a part of yourself—that is, you don't see it at all. Put the thing away for a year, come on it suddenly as a stranger might, and you will perhaps understand why Thomas seemed so cool about it. It wasn't because he was jealous or unfriendly, as you supposed: it was because he *saw* it and you didn't.

Even great men have this blindness about their own work. How else can we account for a case like Wordsworth's? He was one of the three greatest poets this country has produced, and also an acute critic of poetry, yet he wrote more flat-footed commonplace than any man of his time. Apparently he didn't know when he was sublime and when he was merely drivelling. He didn't know because he never got outside the hypnotism of self.

I have sometimes felt angry with that phrase, "What do they know of England, who only England know?" It is the watchword of a shallow Imperialism. But I felt a certain truth in it once. I was alone in the Alps, in an immense solitude of peak and glacier, and as I waited for the return of my guide, who had gone on ahead to prospect, I looked, like Richard, "towards England." In that moment I seemed to see it imaginatively, comprehensively, as I had never, never seen it in all the years of my life in it. I saw its green pastures and moorlands, its mountains and its lakes, its cities and its people, its splendours and its squalors as if it was all a vision projected beyond the verge of the horizon. I saw it with a fresh eye and a new mind, seemed to understand it as I had never understood it before, certainly loved it as I had never loved it before. I found that I had left England to discover it.

That is what we need to do with ourselves occasionally. We need to take a journey from our self-absorbed centre, and see ourselves with a fresh eye and an unprejudiced judgment.

ON THE ENGLISH SPIRIT

I have seen no story of the war which, within its limits, has pleased me more than that which Mr. Alfred Noyes told in the newspapers in his fascinating description of his visit to the Fleet. It was a story of the battle of Jutland. "In the very hottest moment of this most stupendous battle in all history," he says, "two grimy stokers' heads arose for a breath of fresh air. What domestic drama they were discussing the world may never know. But the words that were actually heard passing between them, while the shells whined overhead, were these: 'What I says is, 'e ought to have married 'er.'"

If you don't enjoy that story you will never understand the English spirit. There are some among us who never will understand the English spirit. In the early days of the war an excellent friend of mine used to find a great source of despair in "Tipperary." What hope was there for a country whose soldiers went to battle singing "Tipperary" against a foe who came on singing "Ein' feste Burg"? Put that way, I was bound to confess that the case looked black against us. It seemed "all Lombard Street to a China orange," as the tag of other days would put it. It is true that, for a music-hall song, "Tipperary" was unusually fresh and original. Contrast it with the maudlin "Keep the home fires burning," which holds the field to-day, and it touches great art. I never hear it even now on the street organ without a certain pleasure—a pleasure mingled with pain, for its happy lilt comes weighted with the tremendous emotions of those unforgettable days. It is like a butterfly caught in a tornado, a catch of song in the throat of death.

But it was only a music-hall song after all, and to put it in competition with Luther's mighty hymn would be like putting a pop-gun against a 12-inch howitzer. The thunder of Luther's hymn has come down through four centuries, and it will go on echoing through the centuries till the end of time. It is like the march of the elements to battle, like the heaving of mountains and the surge of oceans. In nothing else is the sense of Power so embodied in the pulse of song. And the words are as formidable as the tune. Carlyle caught their massive, rugged strength in his great translation:

> A safe stronghold our God is still,
> A trusty shield and weapon;
> He'll help us clear from all the ill
> That hath us now o'ertaken....

Yes, on the face of it, it seemed a poor lookout for "Tipperary" against such a foe. But it wasn't, and anyone who knew the English temperament knew it wasn't. I put aside the fact that for practical everyday uses a cheerful tune is much better than a solemn tune. "Tipperary" quickens the step and shortens the march. Luther's hymn, so far from lightening the journey, would become an intolerable burden. The mind would sink under it. You would either go mad or plunge into some violent excess to recover your sanity. It is the craziest of philosophy to think that because you are engaged in a serious business you have to live in a state of exaltation, that the bow is never to be unstrung, that the top note is never to be relaxed. You will not do your business better because you wear a long face all the time; you will do it worse. If you are talking about your high ideals all day you are not only a nuisance: you are either dishonest or unbalanced. We are not creatures with wings. We are creatures who walk. We have to "foot it" even to Mount Pisgah, and the more cheerful and jolly and ordinary we are on the way the sooner we shall get over the journey. The noblest Englishman that ever lived, and the most deeply serious, was as full of innocent mirth as a child and laid his head down on the block with a jest. Let us keep our course by the stars, by all means, but the immediate tasks are much nearer than the stars—

> The charities that soothe and heal and bless
> Are scattered all about our feet—like flowers.

It is just this frightful gravity of the German mind that has made them mad. They haven't learned to play; they haven't learned to laugh at themselves. Their sombre religion has passed into a sombre irreligion. They have grown gross without growing light-hearted. The spiritual battle song of Luther has become a material battle song, and "the safe stronghold" is no longer the City of God but the City of Krupp. They have neither the splendid intellectual sanity of the French, nor the homely humour of the English. It is this homely humour that has puzzled Europe. It has puzzled the French as much as the Germans, for the French genius is declamatory and needs the inspiration of ideas and great passions greatly stated. It was assumed that, because the British soldier sang "Tipperary," moved in an atmosphere of homely fun, indulged in no heroics, never talked of "glory," rarely of patriotism or the Fatherland, and only joked about "the flag," there was no great passion in him. Some of our frenzied people at home have the same idea. They still believe we are a nation of "slackers" because we don't shriek with them.

The truth, of course, is that the English spirit is distrustful of emotion and display. It is ashamed of making "a fuss" and hates heroics. The typical Englishman hides his feelings even from his family, clothes his affections under a mask of indifference, and cracks a joke to avoid "making a fool of himself." It is not that he is without great passions, but that he does not like talking about them. He is too self-conscious to trust his tongue on such big themes. He might "make an exhibition of himself," and he dreads that above all things. This habit of reticence has its unlovely side; but it has great virtues too. It keeps the mind cool and practical and the atmosphere commonplace and good-humoured. It gives reserves of strength that people who live on their "top notes" have not got. It goes on singing "Tipperary" as though it had no care in life and no interest in ideas or causes. And then the big moment comes and the great passion that has been kept in such shamefaced secrecy blazes out in deeds as glorious as any that were done on the plains of windy Troy. Turn to those stories of the winning of the V.C., and then ask yourself whether the nation whose sons are capable of this noble heroism deserves to have the whip of Zabern laid across its shoulders by any jack-in-office who chooses to insult us.

Those two stokers, putting their heads out for a breath of fresh air in the midst of the battle, are true to the English type. Death was all about them, and any moment might be their last. But they were so completely masters of themselves that in the brief-breathing space allowed them they could turn their minds to a simple question of everyday conduct. "What I says is, 'e ought to have married 'er." That is not the stuff of which heroics are made; but it is the stuff of which heroism is made.

ON FALLING IN LOVE

Do not, if you please, imagine that this title foreshadows some piquant personal revelation. "Story! God bless you, I have none to tell, sir." I have not fallen in love for quite a long time, and, looking in the glass and observing what Holmes calls "Time's visiting cards" on my face and hair, I come to the conclusion that I shall never enjoy the experience again. I may say with Mr. Kipling's soldier that

> That's all shuv be'ind me
> Long ago and fur away.

But just as poetry, according to Wordsworth, is emotion recalled in tranquillity, so it is only when you have left the experience of falling in love behind that you are really competent to describe it or talk about it with the necessary philosophic detachment.

Now of course there is no difficulty about falling in love. Any one can do that. The difficulty is to know when the symptoms are true or false. So many people mistake the symptoms, and only discover when it is too late that they have never really had the true experience. Hence the overtime in the Divorce Court. Hence, too, the importance of "calf love," which serves as a sort of apprenticeship to the mystery, and enables you to discriminate between the substance and the shadow.

And in "calf love" I do not include the adumbrations of extreme childhood like those immortalised in *Annabel Lee*:–

> I was a child and she was a child
> In that kingdom by the sea.

> *   *   *   *   *

> But we loved with a love that was more than love,
> I and my Annabel Lee.

I know that love. I had it when I was eight. "She" was also eight, and she had just come from India. She was frightfully plain, but then—well, she had come from India. She had all the romance of India's coral strand about her, and it was India's coral strand that I was in love with. Moreover, she was a soldier's daughter, and to be a soldier's daughter was, next to being a soldier, the noblest thing in the world. For that was about the time when, under the inspiration of *The Story of the Hundred Days*, I had set out with a bag containing a nightshirt and a toothbrush to enlist in the Black Watch. (It was a forlorn adventure that went no further than the railway station.) Finally she had given me, as a token of her love, *Poor Little Gaspard's Drum*, wherein I read of Napoleon and the Egyptian desert, and, above all, of the Mamelukes. How that word thrilled me! "The Mamelukes!" What could one do but fall in love with a girl who used such incantations?

But this is not the true calf love. That comes with the down upon the lip. People laugh at "calf love," but one might as well laugh at the wonder of dawn or the coming of spring. When David Copperfield fell in love with the eldest Miss Larkins, he was really in love with the opening universe, and the eldest Miss Larkins happened to be the only available lightning conductor for his emotion.

The important thing is that you should contract "calf love" while you are young. It is like the measles, which is harmless enough in childhood, but apt to be dangerous when you are grown up. The "calf love" of an elderly man is always a disaster. Hence the saying, "There's no fool like an old fool." An elderly man should not *fall* in love. He should walk into it. He should survey the ground carefully as Mr. Barkis did. That admirable man took the business of falling in love seriously:

"'So she makes,' said Mr. Barkis, after a long interval of reflection, 'all the apple parsties, and does all the cooking, do she?'

"I replied that such was the fact.

"'Well, I'll tell you what,' said Mr. Barkis. 'P'raps you might be writin' to her?'

"'I shall certainly write to her,' I rejoined.

"'Ah!' he said, slowly turning his eyes towards me. 'Well! If you was writin' to her, p'raps you'd recollect to say that Barkis was willin', would you?'"

This is a model of caution in the art of middle-aged love-making. The mistake of the "Northern Farmer" was that he applied the same middle-aged caution to youth. "Doänt thou marry for munny; but goä wheer munny is," he said to his son Sammy, who wanted to marry the poor parson's daughter. And he held up his own love-making as an inspiration for Sammy:

And I went wheer munny wor, and thy moother coom to and
  Wi' lots o' munny laäid by, and a nicetish bit o' land.
  Maybe she worn'd a beauty: I nivver giv' it a thowt;
But worn'd she as good to cuddle and kiss as a lass as an't nowt?

I have always hoped that Sammy rejected his father's counsel and stuck to the poor parson's daughter.

There is no harm of course in marrying money. George Borrow said that there were worse ways of making a fortune than marrying one. And perhaps it is true, though I don't think Borrow's experience was very convincing. I have known people who "have gone where money was" and have fallen honestly and rapturously into love, but you have got to be very sure that money in such a case is not the motive. If it is the penalty never fails to follow. Mr. Bumble married Mrs. Corney for "six teaspoons, a pair of sugar tongs, and a milk-pot, with a small quantity of secondhand furniture and twenty pounds in money." And in two months he regretted his bargain and admitted that he had gone "dirt cheap." "Only two months to-morrow," he said. "It seems a age."

Those who believe in "love at first sight" take the view that marriages are made in heaven and that we only come to earth to fulfil our destiny. Johnson, who was an excellent husband to the elderly Mrs. Porter, scoffed at that view and held that love is only the accident of circumstance. But though that is the sensible view, there are cases like those of Dante and Beatrice and Abelard and Heloise, in which the passion does seem to touch the skies. In those cases, however, it rarely ends happily. A more hum-drum way of falling in love seems better fitted to earthly conditions. The method of Sir Thomas More was perhaps the most original on record. He preferred the second of three sisters and was about to marry her when it occurred to him—But let me quote the words in which Roper, his son-in-law, records the incident:

"And all beit his mynde most served him to the seconde daughter, for that he thoughte her the fayrest and best favoured, yet when he considered that it woulde be bothe great griefe and some shame alsoe to the eldest to see her yonger sister in mariage preferred before her, he then of a certeyn pittye framed his fancye towardes her, and soon after maryed her."

It was love to order, yet there was never a more beautiful home life than that of which this most perfect flower of the English race was the centre.

In short, there is no formula for falling in love. Each one does it as the spirit moves.

ON A BIT OF SEAWEED

The postman came just now, and among the letters he brought was one from North Wales. It was fat and soft and bulgy, and when it was opened we found it contained a bit of seaweed. The thought that prompted the sender was friendly, but the momentary effect was to arouse wild longings for the sea, and to add one more count to the indictment of the Kaiser, who had sent us for the holidays into the country, where we could obey the duty to economise, rather than to the seaside, where the temptations to extravagance could not be dodged. "Oh, how it smells of Sheringham," said one whose vote is always for the East Coast. "No, there is the smack of Sidmouth, and Dawlish, and Torquay in its perfume," said another, whose passion is for the red cliffs of South Devon. And so on, each finding, as he or she sniffed at the seaweed, the windows of memory opening out on to the foam of summer seas. And soon the table was enveloped in a rushing tide of recollection—memories of bathing and boating, of barefooted races on the sands, of jolly fishermen who always seemed to be looking out seaward for something that never came, of hunting for shells, and of all the careless raptures of dawn and noon and sunset by the seashore. All awakened by the smell of a bit of seaweed.

It is this magic of reminiscence that makes the world such a storehouse of intimacies and confidences. There is hardly a bird that sings, or a flower that blows, or a cloud that sails in the blue that does not bring us some hint from the past, and set us tingling with remembrance. We open a drawer by chance, and the smell of lavender issues forth, and with that lingering perfume the past is unrolled like a scroll, and places long unseen leap to the inward eye and voices long unheard are speaking to us:—

> We tread the path their feet have worn.
> We sit beneath their orchard trees,
> We hear, like them, the hum of bees,
> And rustle of the bladed corn.

Who can see the first daffodils of spring without feeling a sort of spiritual festival that the beauty of the flower alone cannot explain? The memory of all the springs of the past is in their dancing plumes, and the assurance of all the springs to come. They link us up with the pageant of nature, and with the immortals of our kind—with Wordsworth watching them in "sprightly dance" by Ullswater, with Herrick finding in them the sweet image of the beauty and transience of life, with Shakespeare greeting them "in the sweet o' the year" by Avon's banks long centuries ago.

And in this sensitiveness of memory to external suggestion there is infinite variety. It is not a collective memory that is awakened, but a personal memory. That bit of seaweed opened many windows in us, but they all looked out on different scenes and reminded us of something individual and inexplicable, of something which is a part of that ultimate loneliness that belongs to all of us. Everything speaks a private language to each of us that we can never translate to others. I do not know what the lilac says to you; but to me it talks of a garden-gate over which it grew long ago. I am a child again, standing within the gate, and I see the red-coated soldiers marching along with jolly jests and snatching the lilac sprays from the tree as they pass. The emotion of pride that these heroes should honour our lilac tree by ravishing its blossoms all comes back to me, together with a flood of memories of the old garden and the old home and the vanished faces. Why that momentary picture should have fixed itself in the mind I cannot say; but there it is, as fresh and clear at the end of nearly fifty years as if it were painted yesterday, and the lilac tree bursting into blossom always unveils it again.

It is these multitudinous associations that give life its colour and its poetry. They are the garnerings of the journey, and unlike material gains they are no burden to our backs and no anxiety to our mind. "The true harvest of my life," said Thoreau, "is something as intangible and indescribable as the tints of morning and evening." It was the summary, the essence, of all his experience. We are like bees foraging in the garden of the world, and hoarding the honey in the hive of memory. And no hoard is like any other hoard that ever was or ever will be. The cuckoo calling over the valley, the blackbird fluting in the low boughs in the evening, the solemn majesty of the Abbey, the life of the streets, the ebb and flow of Father Thames—everything whispers to us some secret that it has for no other ear, and touches a chord of memory that echoes in no other brain. Those deeps within us find only a crude expression in the vehicle of words and actions, and our intercourse with men touches but the surface of ourselves. The rest is "as intangible and indescribable as the tints of morning and evening." It was one of the most companionable of men, William Morris, who said:

> That God has made each one of us as lone
> As He Himself sits.

That is why, in moments of exaltation, our only refuge is silence, and the world of memory within answers the world of suggestion without.

"And what does the seaweed remind you of?" said one, as I looked up after smelling it. "It reminds me," I said, "of all the seas that wash our shores, and of all the brave sailors who are guarding these seas day and night, while we sit here secure. It reminds me also that I have an article to write, and that its title is 'A Bit of Seaweed.'"

ON LIVING AGAIN

A little group of men, all of whom had achieved conspicuous success in life, were recently talking after dinner round the fire in the smoking-room of a London club. They included an eminent lawyer, a politician whose name is a household word, a well-known divine, and a journalist. The talk traversed many themes, and arrived at that very familiar proposition: If it were in your power to choose, would you live this life again? With one exception the answer was a unanimous "No." The exception, I may remark, was not the divine. He, like the majority, had found one visit to the play enough. He did not want to see it again.

The question, I suppose, is as old as humanity. And the answer is old too, and has always, I fancy, resembled that of our little group round the smoking-room fire. It is a question that does not present itself until we are middle-aged, for the thoughts of youth are long, long thoughts, and life then stretches out in such an interminable vista as to raise no question of its recurrence. It is when you have reached the top of the pass and are on the downward slope, with the evening shadows falling over the valley and the church tower and with the end of the journey in view, that the question rises unbidden to the lips. The answer does not mean that the journey has not been worth while. It only means that the way has been long and rough, that we are footsore and tired, and that the thought of rest is sweet. It is nature's way of reconciling us to our common lot. She has shown her child all the pageant of life, and now prepares him for his "patrimony of a little mould"–

> Thou hast made his mouth
> Avid of all dominion and all mightiness,
> All sorrow, all delight, all topless grandeurs,
> All beauty, and all starry majesties,
> And dim transtellar things;–even that it may,
> Filled in the ending with a puff of dust,
> Confess–"It is enough."

Yes, it is enough. We accept the verdict of mortality uncomplainingly–nay, we would not wish it to be reversed, even if that were possible.

Now this question must not be confounded with that other, rather foolish, question, "Is Life worth living?" The group round the smoking-room fire would have answered that question–if they had troubled to answer it at all–with an instant and scornful "Yes." They had all found life a great and splendid adventure; they had made good and wholesome use of it; they would not surrender a moment of its term or a fragment of its many-coloured experience. And that is the case with all healthy-minded people. We may, like Job, in moments of depression curse the day when we were born; but the curse dies on our lips. Swift, it is true, kept his birthday as a day of mourning; but no man who hates humanity can hope to find life endurable, for the measure of our sympathies is the measure of our joy in living.

Even those who take the most hopeless view of life are careful to keep out of mischief. A friend of mine told me recently of a day he had spent with a writer famous for the sombre philosophy of his books. In the morning the writer declared that no day ever passed in which he did not wish that he had never been born; in the afternoon he had a most excellent opportunity of being drowned through some trouble with a sailing boat, and he rejected the chance with almost pathetic eagerness. Yet I daresay he went on believing that he wished he had never been born. It is not only the children who live in the world of "Let us make pretend."

No, we are all glad to have come this way once. It is the thought of a second journey over the same ground that chills us and gives us pause. Sometimes you will hear men answer, "Yes, if I could have the experience I have had in this life." By which they mean, "Yes, if I could come back with the certainty of making all the short cuts to happiness that I now see I have missed." But that is to vulgarise the question. It is to ask that life shall not be a splendid mystery, every day of which is

an arch wherethrough
Gleams the untravelled world;

but that it shall be a thoroughly safe three per cent. investment into which I can put my money with the certainty of having a good time—all sunshine and no shadows. But life on those terms would be the dreariest funeral march of the marionettes. Take away the uncertainty of life, and you take away all its magic. It would be like going to the wicket with the certainty of making as many runs as you liked. No one would trouble to go to the wicket on those preposterous terms. It is because I may be out first ball or stay in and make a hundred runs (not that I ever did any such heroic thing) that I put on the pads with the feverish sense of adventure. And it is because every dawn breaks as full of wonder as the first day of creation that life preserves the enchantment of a tale that is never told.

Moreover, how would experience help us? It is character which is destiny. If you came back with that weak chin and flickering eye, not all the experience of all the ages would save you from futility.

No, if life is to be lived here again it must be lived on the same unknown terms in order to be worth living. We must come, as we came before, like wanderers out of eternity for the brief adventure of time. And, in spite of all the fascinations of that adventure, the balance of our feeling is against repeating it. For we know that everything that makes life dear to us would have vanished with all the old familiar faces and happy

54

associations of our former pilgrimage, and there is something disloyal in the mere thought of coming again to form new attachments and traverse new ways. Holmes once wrote a poem about being "Homesick in heaven"; but it would be still harder to be homesick on earth–to be wandering about among the ghosts of old memories, and trying to recapture the familiar atmosphere of things. We should make new friends; but they would not be the same. They might be better; but we should not ask for better friends: we should yearn for the old ones.

There is a fine passage in Guido Rey's noble book on the "Matterhorn" which comes to my mind as a fitting expression of what I think we feel. He was on his way to climb the mountain, when, on one of its lower slopes, he saw standing lonely in the evening light the figure of a grey-headed man. It was Whymper, the conqueror of the Matterhorn–Whymper grown old, standing there in the evening light and gazing on the mighty rock that he had vanquished in his prime. His climbing days were done, and he sought no more victories on the mountains. He had had his day and was content to stand afar off, alone with his memories, leaving the joy of battle to the young and the ardent. There was not one of those memories that he would be without–save, of course, that terrible experience in the hour of his victory over the Matterhorn. But had you asked him if he was still avid for those topless grandeurs and starry majesties he would have said, "It is enough."

TU-WHIT, TU-WHOO!

There are two voices that are most familiar to me on this hillside. One is the voice of the day, the other of the night. Throughout the day the robin sings his song with unflagging spirit. It is not a very brilliant song, but it is indomitably cheerful. Wet or fine, warm or cold, it goes on through the November day from sunrise to sunset. The little fellow hops about, in his bright red waistcoat, from tree to tree. He flutters to the fence, and from the fence to the garden path, and so to the door and into the kitchen. If you will give him decent encouragement he will come on to your hand and take his meal with absolute confidence in your good faith. Then he will trip away and resume his song on the fence.

There are some people who say hard things about the robin—that he is selfish and "gey ill to live wi'" and so on—but to me he seems the most cheerful and constant companion in nature. He is a bringer of good tidings—a philosopher who insists that we are masters of our fate and that winter is just the time when there is some sense in being an optimist. Anybody, he seems to say, can be an optimist when the days are long and the air is warm and worms are plentiful; but it is just when things are looking a little black and the other fellows begin to grouse that I put on my brightest waistcoat, tune up my best whistle, and come and tell you that the unconquerable soul is greater than circumstance.

The other voice comes when night has descended and the valley below is blotted out by the darkness. Then from the copse beyond the orchard there sounds the mournful threnody of the owl. The day is over, he says, and all is lost. "Tu-whit, tu-whoo." I only am left to tell the end of all things. "Tu-whit, tu-whoo." I've told it all before a thousand times, but you wouldn't believe me. "Tu-whit, tu-whoo." Now, you can't deny it, for the night is dark and the wind is cold and all the earth is a graveyard. "Tu-whit, tu-whoo." Where are the songs of spring and the leaves of summer? "Tu-whit, tu-whoo." Where the red-cheeked apple that hung on the bough and the butterfly that fluttered in the sunshine? All, all are gone. "Tu-whit, tu-whoo ... Tu-whit, tu-whoo ... Tu-whit, tu-whoo...."

A cheerless fellow. Some people find him an intolerable companion. I was talking at dinner in London a few nights ago to a woman who has a house in Sussex, and I found that she had not been there for some time.

"I used to find the owl endurable," said she, "but since the war I have found him unbearable. He hoots all night and makes me so depressed that I feel that I shall go mad."

"And so you come and listen to the owl in London?" I said.

"The owl in London?" she asked.

"Yes," I said, "the owl that hoots in Carmelite Street and Printing House Square."

"Ah," she said, "but he is such an absurd owl. Now the owl down in the country is such a solemn creature."

"He says a very foolish thing
In such a solemn way,"

I murmured.

"Yes, but in the silence and the darkness there doesn't seem any answer to him."

"Madame," I said, "if you will look up at the stars you will find a very complete answer."

I confess that I find the owl not only tolerable but stimulating. I like to hear the pessimist really let himself go. It is the nameless and unformed fears of the mind that paralyse, but when my owl comes along and states the position at its blackest I begin to cheer up and feel defiant and combative. Is this the worst that can be said? Then let us see what the best is, and set about accomplishing it. "The thing is impossible," said the pessimist to Cobden. "Indeed," said that great man. "Then the sooner we set about doing it the better." Oh, oh, say I to my owl, all is lost, is it? You wait till the dawn comes, and hear what that little chap in the red waistcoat has to say about it. He's got quite another tale to tell, and it's a much more likely tale than yours. I shall go to bed and leave you to Gummidge in the trees until the sun comes up and tells you what a dismal fraud you are.

"Tu-whit, tu-whoo," hoots the owl back at me.

Yes, my dear sir, but you said that last night, and you have been saying it every night I have known you, and always the sun comes up and the spring comes round again and the flowers bloom, and the fields are golden with harvest.

"Tu-whit, tu-whoo."

Oh, bother you. You ought to be a *Daily Mail* placard.

No doubt the owl is quite happy in his way. Louis XV. expressed the owlish philosophy when he said, "Let us amuse ourselves by making ourselves miserable." I have no doubt the wretched creature did amuse himself after his fashion. I have always thought that, secretly, Mrs. Gummidge had a roaring time. She really enjoyed being miserable and making everybody about her miserable. I have known such people, and I daresay you have known them, too—people who nurse unhappiness with the passion of a miser. They are having the time of their lives now. They go about saying, "Tu-whit, tu-whoo! The Russians are beaten again, or if they are not beaten they will be. Tu-whit, tu-whoo! We're slackers and slouchers and the Germans are too many for us. Tu-whit, tu-whoo. They're on the way to India and Egypt, and nothing will stop them. All, all is lost." But I notice that they enjoy a beef-steak as much as anybody, and do not refuse their soup though they salt it with their tears.

I like that story of Stonewall Jackson and the owl. The owl was a general, and he rushed up to Jackson in the crisis of the first battle of Bull's Run, crying "All is lost! We're beaten!" "Oh," said Jackson, "if that's so I'd advise you to keep it to yourself." Half-an-hour later the charge of Jackson's brigade had won the battle. I do not know what happened to the owl, but I daresay he went on "Tu-whit-ing" and "Tu-whoo-ing" to the end. The owl can't help being an owl.

Ah, there is little red waistcoat singing on the fence. Let us find a worm for the philosopher....

ON POINTS OF VIEW

As I sat in the garden just now, with a writing-pad on my knee and my mind ranging the heavens above and the earth beneath in search of a subject, my eye fell on a tragedy in progress at my elbow. A small greenfly had got entangled in a spider's web, and was fluttering its tiny wings violently to effect an escape. The filaments of the web were so delicate as to be hardly visible, but they were not too delicate to bear the spider whom I saw advancing upon his prey with dreadful menace. I forgot my dislike of greenflies, and was overcome with a fierce antagonism for the fat fellow who had the game so entirely in his hands. Here, said I, is the Hun encompassing the ruin of poor little Belgium. What chance has the weak and the innocent little creature against the cunning of this rascal, who hangs out his gossamer traps in the breeze and then lies in hiding until his victim is enmeshed and helpless? What justice is there in nature that allows this unequal combat?

By this time the spider had reached the fly and thrown a new filament round him. Then at frightful speed he raced to the top of his web and disappeared in the woodwork of the arbour, drawing the new filament tight round the victim, which continued its flutterings for a little time and then gave up the ghost. At this moment I was called in to lunch, and at the table I told the story of the spider and the fly with undisguised hostility to the spider. "That," said Robert, home from the front–"that is simply a sentimental point of view. My sympathies as a practical person are all with the spider. He is the friend of man, the devourer of insects, the scavenger of the gardens. He helps in the great task of keeping the equilibrium of nature. Moreover," said he, "I have seen you kill greenflies yourself. You killed them because you knew they were a nuisance. Why should you object to the spider doing the same useful work for a living?"

"Ah," said I weakly, "I suppose it is because he does it for a living. Now I ..." "Now, you," interrupted the other, "do it for a living, too, because you want your fruit trees to bear fruit, and your roses to thrive, and your cabbages to prosper. Who more merciless than you on slugs and other pests that fly or crawl? No, no, we are all out for a living, you as much as the spider, the spider as much as the fly." "We are all Huns," said I. "What a detestable world it is." "Not at all," said he. "It's a very jolly world. I drink to the health of the spider."

"And you have no pity for the fly?" I said. "Not a little bit." he replied. "I am on the side of right." "Whose side is that?" I asked. "Mine," said he. "We must all act according to our point of view. That's what the greenfly does. That's what the spider does. We shall never in this world get all the points of view in accord. We shall go on scrambling for a living to the end. Sometimes the greenfly will be on top, sometimes the spider. Look at that cherry-tree in the orchard. A month ago its branches were laden with fruit. Now there is not a cherry to be seen. The blackbirds and the starlings have stripped the tree as clean as a bone. Their point of view is that the cherries are provided for them, and they are right. They know nothing of the laws of property which man makes for his own protection. It's no use going out to them and asking them to look at your title-deeds, and reminding them of the policeman and the laws against larceny. Our moral code is for us, not for them.

"We are all creatures of our own point of view," he went on. "Before Jones next door bought a motor-car he had very bitter feelings about motorists—used to call them road-hogs, said he would tax these 'land-torpedoes' out of existence, and was full of sympathy and pity for the poor children coming from school. Now he drives a car as hard as anybody; blows the hoggiest of horns; and says it's disgraceful the way parents allow their children to play about in the streets. Nothing has changed except his point of view. He has shifted round to another position, and sees things from a new angle of vision. Samuel Butler hit the comedy of the thing off long ago:—

What makes all doctrine plain and clear?
About two hundred pounds a year.
And that which was proved true before
Prove false again? Two hundred more."

"Are our points of view then all dictated by our selfish motives as those of your friend the spider, who has probably by this time gobbled my friend the greenfly?" "No, I do not say that. I think that, comprehending all our private points of view, there is an absolute motive running through human society, call it the world spirit, the mind of the race, or what you will, that is something greater and better than we. The collective motion of humanity is, except in very rare cases, nobler than its individual manifestations. I respond and you respond to an abstract justice, an abstract righteousness, which is purer and better than anything we are capable of. We are all at the bottom, I think, better than our actions paint us, better than our limited points of view permit us to be, and in our illuminated moments we catch a glimpse of that Jacob's ladder that Francis Thompson saw, with ascending angels, at Charing Cross. Someone called Shelley 'an ineffectual angel.' I think most of us are ineffectual angels. Take this tragedy that is filling the world with horror to-day. We are fighting like tigers for our own points of view, but in our hearts we are ashamed of the spectacle, and know that humanity is better than its deeds. One day, perhaps, the ineffectual angel will find his wings and outsoar the spider point of view.... And, by the way, suppose we go and see how the spider is getting on."

We went out into the garden and found the web. But the little green corpse had gone, and the spider was digesting his meal somewhere out of sight.

(*Note*.—This article should be read in connection with that entitled "On the Downs.")

ON BEER AND PORCELAIN

I was reading an American journal just now when I came across the remark that "one would as soon think of drinking beer out of porcelain as of slapping Nietzsche on the back." Drinking beer out of porcelain! The phrase amused me, and set me idly wondering why you don't drink beer out of porcelain. You drink it (assuming that you drink it at all) with great enjoyment out of a thick earthenware mug or a pewter pot or a vessel of glass, but out of china, never. If you were offered a drink of beer out of a china basin or cup you would feel that the liquor had somehow lost its attraction, just as, if you were offered tea out of a pewter pot, you would feel that the drink was degraded and unpleasant. The explanation that the one drink is coarse and the other fine does not meet the case. People drink beer out of glass, and the finer the glass the better they like it. But there is something fundamentally discordant between beer and porcelain.

It is not, I imagine, that porcelain actually affects the taste or quality of the liquor. It is that some subtle sense of fitness is outraged by the association. The harmony of things is jangled. Touch and taste are no longer in sympathy, and we are conscious of a jar to some remote and inexplicable fibre of our being. It is in the realm of the palate that we get the miracle of these affinities and antipathies in their most elementary shape. Who was it who discovered that two such curiously diverse things as mutton and red-currant jelly make a perfect gastronomic chord? By what stroke of inspiration or luck did some unknown cook first see that apple sauce was just the thing to make roast pork sublime? Who was the Prometheus who brought to earth the tidings that a clove was the lover for whom the apple pudding had pined through all the ages?

Seen in the large, this world is just an inexhaustible mine of materials out of which that singular adventurer, man, is eternally bringing to light new revelations of harmony. The musician gathers together the vibrations of the air and discovers the laws of musical agreement, and out of that discovery emerges the stupendous mystery of song. The poet takes words, and out of their rhythms finds the harmonious vehicle for ideas. The scientist sees the apple fall and has the revelation of a universe moving in a symphony before which the mind stands mute and awestruck. The cook takes the pig from the stye and the apple from the tree and makes a pretty lyric for the dinner-table. The Great Adventure, in short, is just this passionate pursuit of the soul of harmony in things, great and small, spiritual and material. We are all in the quest and our captains are those who lead us to the highest peaks of revelation–Bach fashioning that immortal Concerto for Two Violins that takes us out like unsullied children into fields of asphodel; Wordsworth looking out over Tintern Abbey and capturing for us that

> Sense sublime
> Of something far more deeply interfused,

> Whose dwelling is the light of setting suns,
> And the round ocean and the living air,
> And the blue sky and in the mind of man;

Botticelli weaving the magic lines of the *Madonna of the Magnificat* into a harmony that, once deeply felt, seems to dwell in the heart for ever. And you and I, though we are not captains in the adventure, all have our glimpses—glorious moments when the mind sings in tune with circumstance, when the beauty of the world, or the sense of fellowship with men or the anthem of incommunicable things seems to open out the vision of something that we would fain possess and are meant to possess.

"A mirage," you say, being a cynical person—"a mirage just to keep us going through the desert—a sort of carrot held before the nose of that donkey, man." Well, looking at the world to-day, it does rather seem that, if harmony is the main concern of the adventure, humanity had better give up the enterprise. In the light of the events in which we live, man is not merely the most discordant creature on earth: he is also the most ferocious animal that exists. Dryden's famous lines read like a satire:—

> From harmony, from heavenly harmony.
> This universal frame began;
> From harmony to harmony, through all the compass of the
> notes it ran,
> The diapason closing full in man.

If Dryden could see Europe to-day he might at least find one flaw in that ode of which he had so exalted an opinion.

But the story of man is a long story, and we cannot see its drift from any episode, however vast and catastrophic. We are still only in the turbulent childhood of our career, and frightful as our excesses are, there is a motive behind them that makes them profoundly different from the wars of old. That motive is the idea of human liberty, the sanctity of public law, the right of every nation, small or great, to live its life free from the terrorism of force. When, in the ancient or mediaeval world, was there fought a war for a world idea like this? Despotism then had it all its own way. Even the Peace of Rome was only the peace of universal subjugation, not the peace of universal liberty based on law which the world is fighting to establish to-day. Never before has embattled democracy challenged the principle of tyranny for the possession of the world....

Ah, I know what you are thinking as you run your mind over the Allies. Liberty! Does Russia stand for liberty? Yes, in the circumstances of to-day, even Russia stands for liberty, for do not forget that this is not a war of the Russian bureaucracy, but a war sustained by the passion of the Russian people. And, Russia apart or Russia included, who can doubt that the cause of human freedom is in our hands, and the cause of ancient tyranny is in the hands of our enemy? May we not see in these baleful fires the Twilight of the Gods—of those old gods of blood and iron that have held the world in subjection through the long centuries of its travail? May we not see even in the midst of this discord and carnage, this hell of death and destruction, the new birth of humanity—the promise of a world set free?

Perhaps in that distant time when the tragedy of to-day is only an old chapter in the story of the human race it will be seen that Dryden, after all, was not guilty of a grim jest, but that this mighty discord was the announcement of that final harmony for which all that is best in us yearns. It may seem a hard vision to cherish to-day. But we must cherish it, or accept the hideous alternative that this is, after all, in very truth the madhouse of the universe. Can you live with that idea? Would it be worth while living with that idea? If not, then the other holds the field, and it is for all of us in our several ways, small or great, to work so that it may possess the field.

I have wandered somewhat far from the question of the beer and the porcelain, and yet I think you will find that the sequence is not lacking, and that the little window commands a large landscape.

ON A CASE OF CONSCIENCE

It was raining when Victor Crummles stepped out into the street. But he did not notice the fact. True, he put his umbrella up, but that was mere force of habit. He was not aware that he had put it up. His mind was far too engaged with the ordeal before him to permit any consciousness of external things to creep into it. He was "up against it and no mistake," he observed to himself. There was the paper in his pocket telling him the time and place at which he was to present himself for medical examination. He put his hand in his pocket. It was there all right. Kilburn. Twelve o'clock.

Yes, he was fairly up against it. Not, as he hastened to assure himself, that he objected.... Not at all.... He had always been a patriot, and always would be. He'd love to have a smack at the Huns. He'd give them what for.... He wished he'd been a bit younger—that's what he wished. If he'd been a bit younger he'd have gone like a shot. That's what he'd have done—he'd have gone like a shot. No fetching him—if he'd been a bit younger. But a chap at thirty-eight ... well....

Here was the "Golden Crown." Yes, he thought he'd better have "just one." It would pull him together and give the doctors a chance. He ought to give them a chance whatever the consequence to himself. A whisky-and-soda would just put him "in the pink."

There, that was better. Now he could face anything. Now for Kilburn. How should he go? It was two miles at least ... a good two miles. There was No. 16—he could take that. And there was the Tube—he could take that.

Or he could walk. There was plenty of time.... Yes, on the whole he thought he ought to walk. There was that varicose vein. The doctors ought to know about that. It wouldn't be fair to them or to the country that they shouldn't know about it. Varicose veins were very serious affairs indeed. He knew because he'd looked the subject up in the dictionary. It had made such a deep impression on him-that he could repeat what it said:—

"The dilation and thickening of the veins with lengthening and tortuosity, and projection of certain points in the form of knots or knobs, in which the blood coagulates, fibrin is deposited, and in the centre sometimes even osseous matter; in addition the coats of the veins are diseased."

There was more about it than that. It looked a very black case indeed. Many a man had been turned down for varicose veins, and—and—well, the doctors ought to know about it. That was all.... They ought to know about it.... He oughtn't to go there and pass himself off under false pretences.... Mind you, he wanted to fight the Germans all right. He wanted to do his bit—nobody more so. But was it fair not to let the doctors see what was the matter with him? He certainly had those knots and knobs when he walked very hard. Who knew? Perhaps there was "fibrin" and "osseous matter" there. At any rate, the doctors ought to see his leg under fair conditions....

He didn't hold with allowing your patriotism to make you deceive your country. It wasn't fair to the country to let it spend a heap of money on a fellow who might "crock up" in the first week or two. It wasn't fair to the fellow either. Not that he was thinking about himself.... Not at all. It was the country he was thinking of. A fellow must think about the country sometimes. It was his duty to put his own feelings, as it were, under the tap. He wanted to go to the war as much as any man, but he didn't want the country to lose by him....

Yes, it was his duty to walk. It was his duty not to conceal those knots and knobs. He hoped they wouldn't be a fatal objection. But he was going to play a straight bat with the country whatever happened.... He was not the man to palm himself for what he wasn't. He would show the doctor quite plainly what his varicose vein was like.

When Victor Crummles entered the room he was feeling a bit tired, but courageous. He had taken another "stiffener" at the "Spread Eagle" and felt equal to any fate. There were two doctors in the room—one sitting at a table, the other standing by the window.

"Anything the matter with you?" said he at the table.

"Not that I know," said Victor with the air of a man who meant business. Then, as if unwillingly dragging the truth out of himself he added, "I have got a bit of a varicose vein, but it's hardly worth mentioning."

"Oh, don't worry about that," said the doctor. "We've got past that stage. Now strip."

Don't worry about that! Got past that stage! What did it mean?... Well, he had done his duty.... If there was fibrin and osseous matter in his veins he had given them fair warning. It was the country that would suffer. These doctors,... well, there....

"Stripped? Now, let's have a look at you."

The doctor examined him carefully. Perhaps that varicose vein would surprise him after all. He'd walked two miles and it ought to be ... not that he wanted it to be; but if it was—well, it was only fair they should know.

"What did you say your age was?"

"Thirty-eight, sir."

"Thirty-eight! Thirty-eight ... um ... Come here, Jeffkins."

Jeffkins came from the window and joined his colleague, and together the two doctors took stock of Victor. They were taking no notice of his leg. Well, it was their look out. He wouldn't be to blame if he broke down.

"You can dress." And the two doctors went to the window and consulted in low tones.

Then the first came back.

"Well, my man, it won't do," he said. "We like your spirit.... Very creditable, very creditable indeed. But (laughing) thirty-eight! Come, come."

Light was breaking in on Victor. Was he really being rejected?... And because he was too old?... Oh, the scandal, the shame.... And he dying to get at those Huns....

"But upon my oath...." He was really in earnest now.

"There, there, we understand," said the doctor. "You've done your best. And it's very creditable to you—very. But thirty-eight! Come, come.... Now, good morning."

Outside, Victor's anguish and indignation were too bitter to be borne unaided. He turned into the "Spread Eagle."

ON THE GUINEA STAMP

My eye was caught as I passed along the street just now by an advertisement on a hoarding which announced that Mr. Martin Harvey was appearing in a new cinema play entitled *The Hard Way*, which was described as

A FINE STORY BY A PEER

I confess that I took an objection to that play on the spot. It may be a good play. I don't know. I never shall know, for I shall never see it. But why should it be assumed that you and I will run off to the pay box to see a new play "by a peer"? Suppose the anonymous playwright had been a lawyer, or a journalist, or a pork-butcher, or a grocer. Would the producer have thought it helpful to announce a new play by a pork-butcher, or a lawyer, or a grocer, or a journalist? He certainly would not. He would have left the play to stand or fall on its merits.

Why, then, does he think that the fact that it is by a peer will bring us all crowding to his doors? You may, of course, take it as a reflection on the peerage. You may be supposed to think it such a miraculous thing that a peer should be able to write a play that you may be expected to go and see it as you would go to Barnum's to see a two-headed man or a bearded woman? We may be invited to see it merely as a marvel, much as we used to be invited to go and see the horse that could count or the monkeys that could ride bicycles.

If it were so I should feel it was unjust to the peerage which is certainly not below the average in intellectual capacity. But it is not so. It is something much more serious than that. It is not intended to be a reflection on the peerage. It is an unconscious reflection on the British public. The idea behind the announcement is not that we shall go to see the play in a spirit of curiosity, as if it had been written by an ourang-outang, but that we shall go to see it in a spirit of flunkeyism, as if it had been written by a demigod. We are conceived sitting in hushed wonder that a visitor from realms far above our experience should stoop down to amuse us.

I wish I could feel that this was a false estimate of the British public. It would certainly be a false estimate of the French public. The most splendid thing, I think, in connection with the French people is their freedom from flunkeyism. The great wind of the Revolution blew that rubbish out of their souls forever. It gave them the sublime conception of citizenship as the basis of human relationship. It destroyed all the social fences that feudalism had erected to keep the people out of the common inheritance of the possibilities of human life. It liberated them from shams, and made them the one realistic people in Europe. They looked truth in the face, because they had cleaned its face of the dirty accretions of the past. They saw, and they are the only people in Europe who as a nation have seen, that

> The rank is but the guinea stamp:
> The man's the gowd, for a' that.

It is this fact which has made France the standard-bearer of human ideals. It is this fact which puts her spiritually at the head of all the nations.

I am afraid it must be admitted that we are still in the flunkey stage. We are still hypnotised by rank and social caste. I saw a crowd running excitedly after a carriage near the Gaiety Theatre the other day, and found it was because Princess So-and-So was passing. Our Press reeks with the disease, and loves to record this sort of thing:—

THE DUKE OF CONNAUGHT IN NEW YORK.

> While strolling down Fifth Avenue the
> Duke of Connaught accidentally collided
> with a messenger boy carrying a parcel,
> whereupon he turned round and begged the
> boy's pardon.

You see the idea behind such banalities. It is that we are stricken with respectful admiration that people with titles should act like ordinary decent human beings. It is an insult to them, and it ought to be an insult to the intelligence of the reader. But the newspaper man knows his public as well as the cinema producer. He knows we have the souls of flunkeys. I am no better than the rest. When I knew Mr. Kearley, the grocer, I looked on him as a man and an equal. When he blossomed into Lord Devonport I felt that he had taken wings and flown beyond my humble circle. I feel the flunkey strong in me. I hate him, but I cannot kill him.

It is not the fact that inferior people get titles which should give us concern. It is not even that they get them so often by secret gifts, by impudent touting, by base service. These things are known, and they are no worse to-day than they have always been. Every honours list makes us gape and smile. If we see a really distinguished name in it we feel surprise and a certain sorrow. What is he doing in that galley? I confess I have never felt the same towards J.M. Barrie since he allowed a tag to be stuck on to a great name. What did he want with a tag that any tuft hunter in public life can get? It is only littleness that can gain from titles. Greatness is always dishonoured by them. Fancy Sir Charles Dickens, or Lord Dickens, or Lord Darwin, or Lord Carlyle, or Lord Shakespeare, or John Milton masquerading as the Marquis of Oxfordshire. Yes,

Tennyson became a lord and was the smaller man for the fact. Who does not recall Swinburne's scornful comment:

> Stoop, Chaucer, stoop;
> Keats, Shelley, Burns bow down.

And who did not share the feeling of Mark Pattison at the pitiful anti-climax? "There certainly is something about Tennyson," he said, "that you find in very few poets; in saying what he says in the best words in which it can be said, he is quite Sophoclean. But this business of the peerage! It is really so sad that I hardly like to speak of it. Compare that with Milton's ending and mark the difference."

But it is the corrupting effect of titles on the national currency that is their real offence. They falsify our ideals. They set up shams in place of realities. They turn our minds from the gold to the guinea stamp and make us worship the false idols of social ambition. Our thinking as a people can't be right when our symbols are wrong. We can't have the root of democracy in our souls if the tree flowers into coronets and gee-gaws. France has the real jewel of democracy and we have only got the paste. Do not think that this is only a small matter touching the surface of our national character. It is a poison in the blood that infects us with the deadly sins of servility and snobbery. And already it is permeating even the free life of the Colonies. If I were an Australian or a Canadian I would fight this hateful taint of the old world with all my might. I would make it a criminal offence for a Colonial to accept a title. As for us, I know only one remedy. It is to make a title a money transaction. Let us have a tariff for titles. If American millionaires, like Lord Astor, want them let them pay for them at the market rate. It would be at least a more wholesome method than the present system. And it would bring the whole imposture into contempt. Nobody would have a title when everybody knew what he had paid for it. It is a poor way of getting rid of the abomination compared with the French way, but then we are some centuries behind the French people in these things.

ON THE DISLIKE OF LAWYERS

"I have spent a large part of my life in advising business men how to get out of their difficulties," said Mr. Asquith the other day. It was a statement wrung from him by a deputation which was inflicting on him the familiar talk about lawyers and the need of "business men" to run our affairs. I suppose there has been no more banal cackle in this war than the cackle about a "business Government" and the pestilence of lawyers.

I am not a lawyer, and have no particular affection for lawyers. I keep out of their professional reach as much as possible. But it is as foolish to ban them as a class as it would be to assume that a grocer or a tailor is a great statesman because he is a successful grocer or tailor. Running an empire is quite a different job from running a grocery establishment, and it is folly to suppose that because a man has been successful in buying and selling bacon and butter for his own profit he can *ipso facto* govern a nation with wisdom and prudence. Who are the most distinguished grocers of to-day? They are Lord Devonport and Sir Thomas Lipton. Both excellent men, I've no doubt. But would you like to hand over the Premiership to either of them? Now, would you?

The great statesman has to prove himself a great statesman just as the great grocer has to prove himself a great grocer. He has to prove it by the qualities of statesmanship exercised in the full glare of publicity. If the grocer makes a howler in his trade the world knows nothing about it. If the statesman makes a howler all the world knows about it. He has to emerge to the front in the most public of all battles, and you may be sure that no one comes to eminence without great powers which have passed the test of the fiercest trials. He does not evade that test because he is a lawyer. Mr. Asquith had to survive it just as Mr. Chamberlain, who was a maker of nails, had to survive it, just as Mr. Balfour, who is a landowner, had to survive it. No one said to Mr. Chamberlain, "Yah! nailmaker," or to Mr. Balfour, "Yah! landlord," thinking he had disposed of them. Why should you suppose that when you have said "Yah! lawyer" to Mr. Asquith or Mr. Lloyd George you have disposed of them?

Is the idea that lawyers are more selfish than other people—brewers, or soap boilers, or bankers? I doubt it. They are just the average, and include good and bad like any other class. Judge Jeffreys was a monster; but, on the other hand, it was the lawyers of the seventeenth century who largely saved the liberties of this country. I doubt whether the world has ever produced a wiser, more unselfish, more heroic figure than Lincoln. And he was a lawyer. I doubt whether any man in politics to-day has made such financial sacrifices as Mr. Asquith has made. He had a practice at the Bar which, I believe, brought him in £10,000 a year, and had he devoted himself to it instead of to politics, would have brought him in far more, and he gave it up for a job immeasurably more burdensome that has never brought him more than £5000. He might have been Lord

Chancellor, with a comfortable seat on the Woolsack and £10,000 a year, and he chose instead to sit in the House of Commons every day to be the target of every disappointed placeman. Ah, you say, but look at the glory. Well, look at it. I would, as Danton said, rather keep sheep on the hillside than meddle with the government of men. It is the most ungrateful calling on earth. And, whatever other defects may be attributed to Mr. Asquith, a passion for such an empty thing as glory is not one of them. You will discover more passion for glory in Mr. Churchill in five minutes than you will discover in Mr. Asquith in five years. And Mr. Churchill is not a lawyer.

But this dislike of lawyers in the abstract has a certain basis. It is an old dislike. You remember that remark of Johnson's when he was asked on a certain occasion who was the man who had left the room: "I don't like saying unpleasant things about a man behind his back; *but I believe he is an attorney."* And Carlyle was not much more civil when he described a barrister as "a loaded blunderbuss "–if you bought him he blew your opponent's brains out; if your opponent bought him he blew yours out. His weapon is the law, but his object is not justice. As often as not he aims at defeating justice, and the more skilful a lawyer he is the more injustice he succeeds in doing. It is this detachment from the merits of a case, this deliberate repudiation of conscience in his business relations that makes him so suspect. Of course he has a very sound reply. "It is my business to put my client's case, and my opponent's business to put his client's case. And it is the business of the judge and jury to see that justice is done as between us." That is true, but it does not get rid of the suspicion that attaches to a man who fights for the guilty or the innocent with equal fervour.

And then he deals in such a tricky article. When Sancho Panza was Governor of the Island of Barataria he administered justice. If he had been the Governor of the Island of Britain he would have administered the law, and his decisions would have been very different. Law has about the same relation to justice that grammar has to Shakespeare. If Shakespeare were put in the dock and tried by the grammarians he would be condemned as a rogue and vagabond, and, similarly, justice is not infrequently hanged by the lawyers. We must have law just as we must have grammar, but we have no love for either of them. They are dry, bloodless sciences, and we look askance at those who practice them. You may be the greatest rascal of your time, but if you study the law and keep within its letter the strong lance of justice cannot reach you. No, law which is the servant of justice often betrays his master.

But do not let us be unjust. If law to-day is more nearly the instrument of justice than it has ever been, it is the great lawyers to whom we chiefly owe the fact. There are Dodsons and Foggs in the law, but there are also Pyms and Pratts who have upheld the liberties of this country in the teeth of tyrant kings and servile Parliaments.

ON THE CHEERFULNESS OF THE BLIND

I was coming off a Tube train last evening when someone said to me: "Will you please give this gentleman an arm to the lift? He is blind." I did so, and found, as I usually find in the case of the blind, that my companion was uncommonly talkative and cheerful. This gaiety of the blind is a perpetual wonder to me. It is as though the outer light being quenched an inner light of the spirit illuminates the darkness. Outside the night is black and dread, but inside there is warmth and brightness. The world is narrowed to the circle of one's own mind, but the very limitation feeds the flame of the spirit, and makes it leap higher. It was the most famous of blind Englishmen who in the days of his darkness made the blind Samson say:—

> He that hath light within his own clear breast
> May sit i' th' centre and enjoy bright day.

And it has been remarked in many cases in which men have gone blind that their cheerfulness so far from being diminished has by some miracle gained a new strength. In no case of which I have had any knowledge has it apparently had the contrary effect. The zest of living seems heightened. Not long ago Mr. Galsworthy wrote to the *Times* a letter in which he spoke with pity of the unhappiness of the blind, and there promptly descended on him an avalanche of protest from the blind themselves. I suppose there was never a man who seemed to have a more intense pleasure in life than the late Dr. Campbell, the founder of the Normal School for the Blind, who worked wonders in extending the range of the activities of the blind, and himself did such apparently impossible things as riding a bicycle and climbing mountains.

Nor was the case of Mr. Pulitzer, the famous proprietor of the *New York World*, less remarkable. Night came down on him with terrible suddenness. He was watching the sunset from his villa in the Mediterranean one evening when he said: "How quickly the sun has set." "But it has not set," said his companion. "Oh, yes, it has; it is quite dark," he answered. In that moment he had gone stone blind. But I am told by those who knew him that his vivacity of mind was never greater than in the years of his blindness.

My friend Mr. G.W.E. Russell has a theory that the advantage of the blind over the deaf and dumb in this matter of cheerfulness is perhaps more apparent than real. He points out that it is in company that the blind is least conscious of his misfortune, and that the deaf and dumb is most conscious of it. That is certainly the case. In conversation the sightless are on an equality with the seeing, while the deaf and dumb are shut up in a terrible isolation. The fact that they see is not their gain but their loss. They watch the movement of the lips and the signs of laughter, but this only adds to the bitterness of the prison of soundlessness in which they dwell. Hence the appearance of gloom. On the other hand, in solitude the deaf and dumb has the advantage. All the colour and movement of life is before him, while the blind is not only denied that vision of the outside world, but has a restriction of movement that the other does not share. Mr. Russell's conclusion, therefore, is that while the happiest moments of the blind are those when he is observed, the happiest of the deaf and dumb are when he is not observed.

There is some measure of truth in this, but I believe, nevertheless, that the common impression is right, and that, judged by the test of the cheerful acceptance of affliction, the loss of sight is less depressing than the loss of hearing and speech. And this for a very obvious reason. After all, the main interest in life is in easy, familiar intercourse with our fellows. I love to watch a golden sunset, to walk in the high beech woods in spring— or, for that matter, in summer or autumn or winter—to see the apples reddening on the trees, and the hedgerows thick with blackberries. But this is the setting of my drama—the scenery of the play, not the play itself. It is its human contacts that give life its vivacity and intensity. And it is the ear and tongue that are the channels of the cheerful interplay of mind with mind. In that interplay the blind man has full measure and brimming over. His very affliction intensifies his part in the human comedy and gives him a peculiar delight in homely intercourse. He is not merely at his ease in the human family: he is the centre of it. He fulfils Johnson's test of a good fellow: he is "a clubbable man."

And even in the enjoyment of the external world it may be doubted whether he does not find as much mental stimulus as the deaf-and-dumb. He cannot see the sunset, but he hears the shout of the cuckoo, the song of the lark, "the hum of bees, and rustle of the bladed corn." And if, as usually happens, he has music in his soul, he has a realm of gold for his inheritance that makes life a perpetual holiday. Have you heard Mr. William Wolstenholme, the composer, improvising on the piano? If not, you have no idea what a jolly world the world of sounds can be to the blind. Of course, the case of the musician is hardly a fair test. With him, hearing is life and deafness death. There is no more pathetic story than that of Beethoven breaking the strings of the piano in his vain efforts to make his immortal harmonies penetrate his soundless ears. Can we doubt that had he been afflicted with blindness instead of deafness the tragedy of his life would have been immeasurably relieved? What peace, could he have heard his Ninth Symphony, would have slid into his soul. Blind Milton, sitting at his organ, was a less tragic figure and probably a happier man than Milton with a useless ear-trumpet would have been. Perhaps without the stimulus of the organ he could not have fashioned that song which, as Macaulay says in his grandiloquent way, "would not have misbecome the lips of those ethereal beings whom he saw with that inner eye, which no calamity could darken, flinging down on the jasper pavements their crowns of amaranth and gold."

It is probable that in a material sense blindness is the most terrible affliction that can befall us; but I am here speaking only of its spiritual effects, and in this respect the deprivation of hearing and speech seems to involve a more forlorn state than the deprivation of sight. The one affliction means spiritual loneliness: the other deepens the spiritual intimacies of life. It was a man who had gone blind late in life who said: "I am thankful it is my sight which has gone rather than my hearing. The one has shut me off from the sun: the other would have shut me off from life."

ON TAXING VANITY

That quaint idea of Sir Edward Clarke's that, as a revenue expedient in time of war, we should impose a tax on those who have names as well as numbers on their garden gates has a principle in it which is capable of wide extension. It is the principle of taxing us on our vanities. I am not suggesting that there is not also a practical point in Sir Edward's idea. There is no doubt that this custom of giving our houses names is the source of much unnecessary labour and irritation to other people—postmen, tradesmen, debt collectors, and errand boys. Mr. Smythe—formerly Smith—of 236, Belinda Avenue, is easily discoverable, but what are you to do about Mr. Smythe, of Chatsworth House, Belinda Avenue, on a dark night? How are you to find him? There are 350 houses in Belinda Avenue, all as like as two peas, and though Mr. Smythe has a number, he never admits it. Chatsworth House is where he lives, and if you want him it's Chatsworth House that you have to find.

The other night a friend of mine was called to the door at a late hour. It was dark and raining and dismal. At the door stood a coal-heaver. "Please, sir," he said, "can you tell me where Balmoral is? I've got a load of coal to take there, and I've been up and down this road in the dark twice, and can't make out where it is." "It's the fourth house from here to the right," said my friend, and the coal-heaver thanked him and went away. That illustrates the practical case for a tax on house names.

But it was not that case which was in Sir Edward's mind. His view is that we ought to pay for the innocent vanity of living at Chatsworth House instead of 236, Belinda Avenue. Now if that principle is carried into effect, I see no end to its operation. I am not sure that Sir Edward himself would escape. I have often admired his magnificent side-whiskers. I doubt whether there is a pair of side-whiskers to match them in London. That he is proud of them goes without saying. Nobody could possibly have whiskers like them without feeling proud of them. I feel that if I had such whiskers I should never be away from the looking-glass. And consider the pleasurable employment they give in idle moments. Satan, it is said, has mischief still for idle hands to do. But no one with such streamers as Sir Edward's can ever have idle hands. When you have nothing else to do with them you stroke your whiskers and purr. Certainly they are worth paying for. I think they would be dirt cheap at a tax of £1 a side.

And then there are white spats. I don't know how you regard white spats, but I never see them without feeling that something ought to be done about it. I daresay the people who wear them are quite nice people, but I think they ought to suffer in some way for the jolt they give to the sensibilities of humbler mortals who could no more wear white spats than they could stand on their head in the middle of Fleet Street. I am aware that white spats are often only a sort of business advertisement. I have known careers founded on a pair of white spats. There is Simpkins, for example. I remember

75

quite well when he first came to the club in white spats. We all smiled and said it was like Simpkins. He was pushful, meant to get on, and had set up white spats as a part of his stock-in-trade. We knew Simpkins, of course, and discounted the white spats; but they made a great impression on his clients, and he forged ahead from that day. Now he wears a fur-lined coat, drives his own motor-car, and has a man in livery to receive you at the door. But the foundation of his fortunes were the white spats. He understood that maxim of Rochefoucauld that "to succeed in the world you must appear to have succeeded already," and the white spats did the trick. I think he ought to pay for them—£2 a spat is my figure.

Most of us, too, I think, will agree that, if vanity is to be taxed, the wearing of an eyeglass cannot be overlooked. It is impossible to dissociate vanity from the use of the monocle. There are some people, it is true, who wear an eyeglass naturally and unaffectedly, as though they were really born with it and had forgotten that it was there. I saw a lady in a bus the other day who used an eyeglass and yet carried it so well, with such simple propriety and naturalness, that you could not feel that there was any vanity in the matter. But that is an exception. Ordinarily the wearing of a monocle seems like an announcement to the world that you are a person of consequence. Disraeli knew that. His remark, when Chamberlain made his first appearance in the House, that "at least he wore his eyeglass like a gentleman," showed that he knew that, in general, it was an affectation. It was so in his own case, of course. I hope Sir Edward Clarke will agree that £5 is a reasonable tariff for an eyeglass.

There are a thousand other vanities more or less innocent, that will occur to you in looking round. I should put a very stiff tax on painted cheeks and hair-dyes. Any lady dyeing her hair once would be taxed £5 for the privilege. If, growing tired of auburn, she decided to change again to a raven hue, she would pay £10. The tax, in fact, might be doubled for every change of colour. If rather than pay the tax Mrs. Fitzgibbons Jones resolves to wear her hair as nature arranged that she should, life will be simplified for me. The first time I met Mrs. Fitzgibbons Jones she had black hair. A year later I met her husband with a lady with chestnut hair. He introduced me to her as his wife, and she said we had met before. I said I thought she was mistaken, and it was not until we had parted that I realised that it was the same lady with another head of hair and another system of coloration altogether.

The weak point about Sir Edward's idea as a financial expedient is that so few of our vanities would survive the attention of the tax-collector. Personally, I should have the name-plate off my gate at once. Indeed, I'm not sure I'll not have it off as it is. It was there when I came, and I have always been a little ashamed of its foppery, and have long used only the number. Now the name seems rather more absurd than ever. Its pretentiousness is out of tune with these times. I think many of us are getting ashamed of our little vanities without the help of the tax-collector.

ON THOUGHTS AT FIFTY

Stevenson, it will be remembered, once assigned his birthday to a little girl—or was it a boy?—of his acquaintance. The child was fond of birthdays, while he had reached a time of life when they had ceased to have any interest for him. Most of us, if we live long enough, experience that indifference. The birthday emotion vanishes with the toys that awaken it. I remember when life was a journey from one birthday to another, the tedium of which was only relieved by such agreeable incidents as Christmas, Easter, and the school holidays. But for many years I have stumbled up against my birthday, as it were, with a shock of surprise, have given it a nod of recognition as one might greet an ancient acquaintance with whom one has lost sympathy, and have passed on without a further thought about the occasion.

But to-day it is different. One cannot pass over one's fiftieth birthday without feeling that an event has happened. Fifty! Why, the Psalmist's limit is only seventy. Fifty from seventy. An easy sum, but what an impressive answer! Twenty years, and they the years of the sere, the yellow leaf. Only twenty more times to hear the cuckoo calling over the valley and see the dark beech woods bursting into tender green. I look back twenty years, and it seems only a span. And yet how remote fifty seemed in those days! It was so remote as to be hardly worth thinking about. To be fifty was to be among the old fellows, to be on the shelf, to have become an antiquity.

And now here am I at fifty, and so far from feeling like an antiquity, I feel as much of a young fellow as at any time of my life. I had feared that when middle age overtook me I should feel middle-aged and full of sad longings for the old toys and the old pleasures. How would life be tolerable when cricket, for example, had ceased to play an important part in it? Never again to have the ecstasy of a drive along "the carpet" to the boundary or, with a flash of the arm, snapping an opponent in the slips. What a dreary desolation life must be, stripped of those joys! And on the contrary I find that the spirit of youth is no more dependent on cricket than it is on the taste for lollipops. It consists in the contented acceptance of the things that are possible to us. Do not suppose, young fellow, that you are any younger than I am because you can jump five feet eight and I have ceased to want to jump at all. The feeling of youth is something much deeper and more enduring than the ability to jump five feet eight. It may be as vigorous at eighty as it is at eighteen. It is only its manner of expression which is changed. Holmes never admitted that he had grown old. "I am eighty-three young to-day," he would say. And Johnson, with his old age and his infirmities, still insisted that he was "a young fellow"—as, indeed, he was, for where shall we find such freshness of spirit, such a defiance of the tooth of Time as in that grand old boy?

Youth, in fact, is not a physical affair at all, but an affair of the soul. You may be spiritually bald-headed at twenty-five or a romping young blade at eighty. Byron was only thirty-four when he wrote:—

> I am ashes where once I was fire.
> And the soul in my bosom is dead;
> What I loved I now merely admire,
> And my heart is as grey as my head.

Perhaps there was some affectation in this, for Byron was always dramatising himself. But that he died an old man at thirty-six is as indisputable as that Browning died a young man at seventy-seven, with that triumphant envoi of *Asolando* as his last expression of the eternal youth of the soul.

In thinking of old age, the mistake is to assume that the spirit must decay with the body. Of course, if the body is maltreated it will react on the spirit. But the natural decline of the physical powers leaves the healthy spirit untouched with age, should indeed leave it strengthened—glowing not with passion but with a steadier fire. When we are young in years our eager spirit cries for the moon.

> We look before and after,
> And pine for what is not.

But as we get older we learn to be satisfied with something nearer than the moon. The horizon of our hopes and ambitions narrows, but the sky above is not less deep, and we make the wonderful discovery that the things that matter are very near to us. It is the homing of the spirit. We have been avid of the "topless grandeurs" of life, and we return to find that the spiritual satisfactions we sought were all the time within very easy reach. And in cultivating those satisfactions intensively we make another discovery. We find that this is the true way to the "topless grandeurs" themselves, for those topless grandeurs are not without us but within.

But I am afraid I am sermonising, and I do not want to sermonise, though if ever a man may be allowed to sermonise it is when he is completing his half-century. Let me as an antidote recall a little story which the present Bishop of Chester once told me over the dinner table, for it contains a practical recipe for keeping the heart young. He was in his earlier days associated with Archdeacon Jones of Liverpool. The Archdeacon, then over eighty, had been tutor to Gladstone, and one day the future Bishop turned the conversation into a reminiscent channel, and sought to evoke the Archdeacon's memories of the long past. Presently the Archdeacon abruptly changed the subject by asking, "What was the concert of the Philharmonic like last night?" And then, in answer to the obvious surprise which the question had aroused, he added, "Although I am an old man, I want to keep my heart young, and the best way of doing that is not to let one's thoughts live in the past, but to keep them in tune with the life around one."

The truth is that every stage of the journey has its own interests. Probably none is better than another, but my own preference has always been for that stage which I happen to be doing at the time. When I was twenty I thought there was no age like twenty, and now I am fifty I have transferred my enthusiasm to fifty. There is no age like it, I feel, for all-round enjoyment. And I have a strong conviction that if I have the good fortune to reach sixty I shall be found declaring that there is no age like sixty. And why not? It is pleasant to see the sun on the morning hills, but it is not less pleasant to walk home when the shadows are lengthening and the cool of the evening has come.

THE ONE-EYED CAT

"There's Peggy with that horrid cat again—the one-eyed cat from over the fence." I looked out as I heard the ejaculation, and there in truth coming down the garden path was Peggy bearing affectionately in her arms the one-eyed cat from over the fence. Peggy likes the animal in spite of its one eye. I am not sure that she does not like it all the more because of its one eye. I think she has an idea that if she nurses the cat it forgets that it has only one eye and recovers its happiness. She has a passion for all four-legged creatures. I have seen her spend a whole day picking handfuls of grass in the orchard and running with them to the donkey or the horse standing patiently in the neighbour's paddock, and when she hasn't animals to play with she will put a horseshoe on each hand and each foot, and then you will hear from above the plod-plod-plod of a horse going its daily round. But while she has a comprehensive affection for all four-legged things, her most fervent love is reserved for the halt and the blind.

It is only among children that we find the quality of charity sufficiently strong to forgive deformity. The natural instinct is to turn away from any physical imperfection. It is the instinct of the race for the preservation of its forms. We call these forms beauty and the departure from them ugliness, and it is from "beauty's rose," as Shakespeare says, that "we desire increase." If you shudder at the touch of a withered hand or at the sight of a one-eyed cat, it is because you feel that they are a menace to the established forms of life. You are unconsciously playing the part of policeman for nature. You are the guardian of its traditions when you blush at the glance of two eyes and shudder at the glance of one.

And yet it is not impossible to fall in love with the physically defective and sincerely to believe that they are beautiful. Take that incident mentioned by Descartes. He said that when he was a child he used to play with a little girl who had a squint, and that to the end of his days he liked people who squinted. In this case it was the associations of memory that gave a glamour to deformity and made it beautiful. The squint brought back to him the memory of the Golden Age, and through the mist of that memory it was transmuted into loveliness.

Nor is it memory alone that will work the miracle. Intellectual sympathy will do it, too. Wilkes was renowned for his ugliness, but he claimed that, given half an hour's start, he would win the smiles of any woman against any competitor. And when one of his lady admirers, engaged in defending him, was reminded that he squinted badly, she replied: "Of course he does; but he doesn't squint more than a man of his genius ought to squint." Nor was it women alone whom the fellow fascinated. Who can forget the scene when Tom Davies brought him into the company of Dr. Johnson, who hated Wilkes' Radicalism, and would never willingly have consented to meet him? For a time

Johnson refused to unbend, but at last he could hold out no longer, and fell a victim to the charm of Wilkes' talk.

In the same way, Johnson believed his wife to be a woman of perfect beauty. To the rest of the world she was extraordinarily plain and commonplace, but to Johnson she was the mirror of beauty. "Pretty creature," he would say with a sigh in referring to her after her death.

And there, I fancy, we touch the root of the matter. The sense of beauty is in one respect an affair of the soul, and only superficially an aesthetic quality. We start with a common prejudice in favour of certain physical forms. They are the forms with which nature has made us familiar, and we seek to perpetuate them. But if the conventionally beautiful form is allied with spiritual ugliness it ceases to be beautiful to us, and if the conventionally ugly form is allied with spiritual beauty that beauty irradiates the physical deficiency. The soul dominates the senses. Francis Thompson expresses the idea very beautifully when he says:–

> I cannot tell what beauty is her dole,
> Who cannot see her features for her soul.
> As birds see not the casement for the sky.

But there is another sense in which beauty is the most matter-of-fact thing. I can conceive that if the human family had developed only one eye, and that planted in the centre of the forehead, the appearance of a person with two eyes would be as offensive to our sense of beauty as a hand that consisted not of fingers but of thumbs. We should go to the show to see the two-eyed man with just the same feelings as we go now to see the bearded woman. We should not go to admire his two eyes, any more than we go to admire the beard; we should go to enjoy a pleasant sense of disgust at his misfortune and a comfortable satisfaction at the fact that we had not been the victims of such a calamity. We should roll our single eye with a proud feeling that we were in the true line of beauty, from which the two-eyed man in front was a hideous and fantastic departure.

Beauty, in short, is only a tribute which we pay to necessity. In equipping itself for the struggle for existence humanity has found that it is convenient to have two eyes and a stereoscopic vision, just as it is convenient to have four fingers on the hand and one thumb instead of five thumbs. Our members have been developed in the manner best fitted to enable us to fight our battle. And the more perfectly they fulfil that supreme condition the more beautiful we declare them to be. Our ideas of beauty, therefore, are not absolute; they are conditional. They are the humble servants of our necessity. Two eyes are necessary for us to get about our business, and so we fall in love with two eyes, and the more perfect they are for their work the more we fall in love with them, and the more beautiful we declare them to be.

I think that Peggy, nursing her one-eyed cat there in the sun, has not yet accepted our creed of beauty. She will be as conventional as the rest of us when her frocks are longer.

ON THE PHILOSOPHY OF HATS

The other day I went into a hatter's to get my hat ironed. It had been ruffled by the weather, and I had a reason for wishing it to look as new and glossy as possible. And as I waited and watched the process of polishing, the hatter talked to me on the subject that really interested him—that is, the subject of hats and heads.

"Yes," said he, in reply to some remark I had made; "there's a wonderful difference in the shape of 'eads *and* the size. Now your 'ead is what you may call an ord'nary 'ead. I mean to say," he added, no doubt seeing a shadow of disappointment pass across my ordinary face, "I mean to say, it ain't what you would call extry-ord'nary. But there's some 'eads—well, look at that 'at there. It belongs to a gentleman with a wonderful funny-shaped 'ead, long and narrer and full of nobbles—'stror'nary 'ead 'e 'as. And as for sizes, it's wonderful what a difference there is. I do a lot of trade with lawyers, and it's astonishing the size of their 'eads. You'd be surprised. I suppose it's the amount of thinking they have to do that makes their 'eads swell. Now that 'at there belongs to Mr. —— (mentioning the name of a famous lawyer), wonderful big 'ead 'e 'as—7-1/2—that's what 'e takes, and there's lots of 'em takes over 7.

"It seems to me," he went on, "that the size of the 'ead is according to the occupation. Now I used to be in a seaport town, and I used to serve a lot of ships' captains. 'Stror'nary the 'eads they have. I suppose it's the anxiety and worry they get, thinking about the tides and the winds and the icebergs and things...."

I went out of the shop with my ord'nary 'ead, conscious of the fact that I had made a poor impression on the hatter. To him I was only a 6-7/8 size, and consequently a person of no consequence. I should have liked to point out to him that it is not always the big heads that have the jewel in them. Of course, it is true that great men often have big heads. Bismarck's size was 7-1/4, so was Gladstone's, so was Campbell-Bannerman's. But on the other hand, Byron had a small head, and a very small brain. And didn't Goethe say that Byron was the finest brain that Europe had produced since Shakespeare? I should not agree in ordinary circumstances, but as a person with a smallish head, I am prepared in this connection to take Goethe's word on the subject. As Holmes points out, it is not the size of the brain but its convolutions that are important (I think, by the way, that Holmes had a small head). Now I should have liked to tell the hatter that though my head was small I had strong reason to believe that the convolutions of my brain were quite top-hole.

I did not do so and I only recall the incident now because it shows how we all get in the way of looking at life through our own particular peep-hole. Here is a man who sees all the world through the size of its hats. He reverences Jones because he takes 7-1/2; he dismisses Smith as of no account because he only takes 6-3/4. In some degree, we all have this restricted professional vision. The tailor runs his eye over your clothes and reckons you up according to the cut of your garments and the degree of shininess they display. You are to him simply a clothes-peg and your merit is in exact ratio to the clothes you carry. The bootmaker looks at your boots and takes your intellectual, social and financial measurement from their quality and condition. If you are down-at-the-heel, the glossy condition of your hat will not alter his opinion about you. The hat does not come in his range of vision. It is not a part of his criteria.

It is so with the dentist. He judges all the world by its teeth. One look in your mouth and he has settled and immovable convictions about your character, your habits, your physical condition, your position, and your mental attributes. He touches a nerve and you wince. "Ah," says he to himself, "this man takes too much alcohol and tobacco and tea and coffee." He sees the teeth are irregular. "Poor fellow," he says, "how badly he was brought up!" He observes that the teeth are neglected. "A careless fellow," he says. "Spends his money on follies and neglects his family I'll be bound." And by the time he has finished with you he feels that he could write your biography simply from the evidence of your teeth. And I daresay it would be as true as most biographies—and as false.

In the same way, the business man looks at life through the keyhole of his counting-house. The world to him is an "emporium," and he judges his neighbour by the size of his plate glass. And so with the financier. When one of the Rothschilds heard that a friend of his who had died had left only a million of money he remarked: "Dear me, dear me! I thought he was quite well off." His life had been a failure, because he had only put a million by for a rainy day. Thackeray expresses the idea perfectly in *Vanity Fair*:—

"You see," said old Osborne to George, "what comes of merit and industry and judicious speculations and that. Look at me and my banker's account. Look at your poor grandfather Sedley and his failure. And yet he was a better man than I was, this day twenty years—a better man I should say by twenty thousand pounds."

I fancy I, too, have my professional way of looking at things, and am disposed to judge men, not by what they do but by the skill they have in the use of words. And I know that when an artist comes into my house he "sizes me up" from the pictures on the wall, just as when the upholsterer comes he "places" me according to the style of the chairs and the quality of the carpet, or as when the gourmet comes he judges by the cooking and the wine. If you give him champagne he reverences you; if hock he puts you among the commonplace.

In short, we all go through life wearing spectacles coloured by our own tastes, our own calling, and our own prejudices, measuring our neighbours by our own tape-measure, summing them up according to our own private arithmetic. We see subjectively, not objectively; what we are capable of seeing, not what there is to be seen. It is not wonderful that we make so many bad guesses at that prismatic thing, the truth.

ON SEEING LONDON

I see that the *Spectator*, in reviewing a new book on the Tower, says that, whilst visitors to London usually visit that historic monument, Londoners themselves rarely visit it. There is, I suppose, a good deal of truth in this. I know a man who was born in London, and has spent all his working life in Fleet Street, who confesses that he has never yet been inside the Tower. It is not because he is lacking in interest. He has been to St. Peter's at Rome, and he went to Madrid largely to see the Prado. If the Tower had been on the other side of Europe, I think he would probably have made a pilgrimage to it, but it has been within a stone's-throw of him all his life, and therefore he has never found time to visit it.

It is so, more or less, with most of us. Apply the test to yourself or to your friends who live in London, and you will probably be astonished at the number of precious things that you and they have not seen—not because they are so distant, but because they are so near. Have you been to the Record Office, for example? I haven't, although it is within a couple of hundred yards of where I work and although I know it is rich in priceless treasures. I am always going, but "never get," as they say in Lancashire. It is too handy.

I was talking the other day to a City merchant who lives at Sydenham, and who has never seen Hampstead Heath. He had been travelling from Sydenham to the City for a quarter of a century, and has worn the rut so deep that he cannot get out of it, and has hardly more likelihood of seeing the Northern Heights than of visiting the mountains of the moon. Yet Hampstead Heath, which he could see in a morning for the cost of a threepenny ride in the Tube, is one of the incomparable things of Nature. I doubt whether there is such a wonderful open space within the limits of any other great city. It has hints of the seaside and the mountain, the moor and the down in most exquisite union, and the Spaniards Road is as noble a promenade as you will find anywhere.

This incuriousness is not a peculiarity of Londoners only. It is a part of that temporising habit that afflicts most of us. If a thing can be done at any time, then that is just the thing that never gets done. If my Fleet Street friend knew that the Tower was going to be blown to pieces by a Zeppelin to-morrow he would, I am sure, rush off to see it this afternoon. But he is conscious that he has a whole lifetime to see it in, and so he will never see it. We are most of us slackers at the bottom, and need the discipline of a timetable to keep us on the move. If I could put off writing this article till to-morrow I should easily convince myself that I hadn't time to write it to-day.

The point is very well expressed in that story of the Pope who received three American visitors in turn. "How long are you staying?" he said to the first. "Six months, your Holiness," was the reply. "You will be able to see something of Rome in that time," said the Pope. The second was staying three months. "You will see a great deal of Rome in three months," said the Pope. The third was only staying three weeks. "You'll see all there is to be seen in Rome in three weeks," was the Pope's comment. He was a good judge of human nature.

But if we Londoners are no worse than most people we certainly miss more, for there is no such book of revelation as this which we look at so differently. I love to walk its streets with those who know its secrets. Mr. John Burns is such a one. The very stones begin to be eloquent when he is about. They pour out memories at his invitation as the rock poured out water at the touch of Moses. The houses tell you who built them and who lived hi them and where their stone came from. The whole pageant of history passes before you, and you see the spot where Julius Caesar crossed the river at Battersea—where else should he cross?—you discover, it may be for the first time, the exquisite beauty of Waterloo Bridge, and learn what Canovas said about it. York Gate tells you of the long past when the Embankment was not, and when great nobles came through that archway to take the boat for Westminster or the Tower. He makes you dive out of the Strand to see a beautiful doorway, and out of Fleet Street to admire the Henry room. Every foot of Whitehall babbles its legends; you see Tyburn as our forefathers saw it, and George Fox meeting Cromwell there on his return from Ireland. In Westminster Hall he is at his best. You feel that he knew Rufus and all the masons who built that glorious fabric. In fact, you almost feel that he built it himself, so vividly does its story live in his mind and so strong is his sense of possession.

If I were a Dictator I would make him the Great Showman of London. I would have him taking us round and inspiring us with something of his own delight in our astonishing City. We should no longer look upon London then as if it were a sort of Bradshaw's Guide: we should find it as fascinating as a fairy tale, as full of human interest as a Canterbury Pilgrimage. We should never go to Snow Hill without memories of Fagin, or to Eastcheap without seeing Falstaff swaggering along its pavements. Bread Street would resound to us with the tread of young Milton, and Southwark with the echoes of Shakespeare's voice and the jolly laughter of the Pilgrims at the Tabard. Hogarth would accompany us about Covent Garden, and out of Bolt Court we should see the lumbering figure of Johnson emerging into his beloved Fleet Street. We would sit by the fountain in the Temple with Tom Pinch, and take a wherry to Westminster with Mr. Pepys. We should see London then as a great spiritual companionship, in which it is our privilege to have a fleeting part.

ON CATCHING THE TRAIN

Thank heaven! I have caught it.... I am in a corner seat, the compartment is not crowded, the train is about to start, and for an hour and a half, while we rattle towards that haven of solitude on the hill that I have written of aforetime, I can read, or think, or smoke, or sleep, or talk, or write as I choose. I think I will write, for I am in the humour for writing. Do you know what it is to be in the humour for writing—to feel that there is a head of steam somewhere that must blow off? It isn't so much that you have something you want to say as that you must say something. And, after all, what does the subject matter? Any peg will do to hang your hat on. The hat is the thing. That saying of Rameau fits the idea to perfection. Someone was asking that great composer if he did not find difficulty in selecting a subject. "Difficulty? A subject?" said Rameau. "Not at all. One subject is as good as another. Here, bring me the *Dutch Gazette*."

That is how I feel now, as the lights of London fade in our wake and the fresh air of the country blows in at the window. Subject? Difficulty? Here bring me the *Dutch Gazette*. But while any subject would serve there is one of particular interest to me at this moment. It came into my mind as I ran along the platform just now. It is the really important subject of catching trains. There are some people who make nothing of catching trains. They can catch trains with as miraculous an ease as Cinquevalli catches half-a-dozen billiard-balls. I believe they could catch trains in their sleep. They are never too early and never too late. They leave home or office with a quiet certainty of doing the thing that is simply stupefying. Whether they walk, or take a bus, or call a taxi, it is the same: they do not hurry, they do not worry, and when they find they are in time and that there's plenty of room they manifest no surprise.

I have in mind a man with whom I once went walking among the mountains on the French-Italian border. He was enormously particular about trains and arrangements the day or the week before we needed them, and he was wonderfully efficient at the job. But as the time approached for catching a train he became exasperatingly calm and leisured. He began to take his time over everything and to concern himself with the arrangements of the next day or the next week, as though he had forgotten all about the train that was imminent, or was careless whether he caught it or not. And when at last he had got to the train, he began to remember things. He would stroll off to get a time-table or to buy a book, or to look at the engine—especially to look at the engine. And the nearer the minute for starting the more absorbed he became in the mechanism of the thing, and the more animated was his explanation of the relative merits of the P.L.M. engine and the North-Western engine. He was always given up as lost, and yet always stepped in as the train was on the move, his manner aggravatingly unruffled, his talk pursuing the quiet tenor of his thought about engines or about what we should do the week after next.

Now I am different. I have been catching trains all my life, and all my life I have been afraid I shouldn't catch them. Familiarity with the habits of trains cannot get rid of a secret conviction that their aim is to give me the slip if it can be done. No faith in my own watch can affect my doubts as to the reliability of the watch of the guard or the station clock or whatever deceitful signal the engine-driver obeys. Moreover, I am oppressed with the possibilities of delay on the road to the station. They crowd in on me like the ghosts into the tent of King Richard. There may be a block in the streets, the bus may break down, the taxi-driver may be drunk or not know the way, or think I don't know the way, and take me round and round the squares as Tony Lumpkin drove his mother round and round the pond, or—in fact, anything may happen, and it is never until I am safely inside (as I am now) that I feel really happy.

Now, of course this is a very absurd weakness. I ought to be ashamed to confess it. I am ashamed to confess it. And that is the advantage of writing under a pen name. You can confess anything you like, and nobody thinks any the worse of you. You ease your own conscience, have a gaol delivery of your failings—look them, so to speak, straight in the face, and pass sentence on them—and still enjoy the luxury of not being found out. You have all the advantages of a conviction without the nuisance of the penalty. Decidedly, this writing under a pen name is a great easement of the soul.

It reminds me of an occasion on which I was climbing with a famous rock climber. I do not mind confessing (over my pen name) that I am not good on rocks. My companion on the rope kept addressing me at critical moments by the name of Saunders. My name, I rejoice to say, is not Saunders, and he knew it was not Saunders, but he had to call me something, and in the excitement of the moment could think of nothing but Saunders. Whenever I was slow in finding a handhold or foothold, there would come a stentorian instruction to Saunders to feel to the right or the left, or higher up or lower down. And I remember that I found it a great comfort to know that it was not I who was so slow, but that fellow Saunders. I seemed to see him as a laborious, futile person who would have been better employed at home looking after his hens. And so in these articles, I seem again to be impersonating the ineffable Saunders, of whom I feel at liberty to speak plainly. I see before me a long vista of self-revelations, the real title of which ought to be "The Showing Up of Saunders."

But to return to the subject. This train-fever is, of course, only a symptom. It proceeds from that apprehensiveness of mind that is so common and incurable an affliction. The complaint has been very well satirised by one who suffered from it. "I have had many and severe troubles in my life," he said, "*but most of them never happened.*" That is it. We people who worry about the trains and similar things live in a world of imaginative disaster. The heavens are always going to fall on us. We look ahead, like Christian, and see the lions waiting to devour us, and when we find they are only poor imitation lions, our timorous imagination is not set at rest, but invents other lions to scare us out of our wits.

And yet intellectually we know that these apprehensions are worthless. Experience has taught us that it is not the things we fear that come to pass, but the things of which we do not dream. The bolt comes from the blue. We take elaborate pains to guard our face, and get a thump in the small of the back. We propose to send the fire-engine to Ulster, and turn to see Europe in flames. Cowper put the case against all "fearful saints" (and sinners) when he said:

> The clouds ye so much dread
> Are big with mercy, and will break
> With blessings on your head.

It is the clouds you don't dread that swamp you. Cowper knew, for he too was an apprehensive mortal, and it is only the apprehensive mortal who really knows the full folly of his apprehensiveness.

Now, save once, I have never lost a train in my life. The exception was at Calais when the Brussels express did, in defiance of the time-table, really give me and others the slip, carrying with it my bag containing my clothes and the notes of a most illuminating lecture. I chased that bag all through Northern France and Belgium, inquiring at wayside stations, wiring to junctions, hunting among the mountains of luggage at Lille.

It was at Lille that—But the train is slowing down. There is the slope of the hillside, black against the night sky, and among the trees I see the glimmer of a light beckoning me as the lonely lamp in Greenhead Ghyll used to beckon Wordsworth's Michael. The night is full of stars, the landscape glistens with a late frost: it will be a jolly two miles' tramp to that beacon on the hill.

IN PRAISE OF CHESS

I sometimes think that growing old must be like the end of a tiring day. You have worked hard, or played hard, toiled over the mountain under the burning sun, and now the evening has come and you sit at ease at the inn and ask for nothing but a pipe, a quiet talk, and so to bed. "And the morrow's uprising to deeds shall be sweet." You have had your fill of adventure for the day. The morning's passion for experience and possession is satisfied, and your ambitions have shrunk to the dimensions of an easy chair.

And so I think it is with that other evening when the late blackbird is fluting its last vesper song and the toys of the long day are put aside, and the plans of new conquests are waste-paper. I remember hearing Sir Edward Grey saying once how he looked forward to the time when he would burn all his Blue-books and mulch his rose-trees with the ashes. And Mr. Belloc has given us a very jolly picture of the way in which he is going to spend his evening:

> If I ever become a rich man,
> Or if ever I grow to be old,
> I will build a house with deep thatch
> To shelter me from the cold,
> And there shall the Sussex songs be sung
> And the story of Sussex told.
> I will hold my house in the high woods
> Within a walk of the sea,
> And the men that were boys when I was a boy
> Shall sit and drink with me.

There is Mr. Birrell, too, who, as I have remarked elsewhere, once said that when he retired he would take his modest savings into the country "and really read Boswell."

These are typical, I suppose, of the dreams that most of us cultivate about old age. I, too, look forward to a cottage under the high beech woods, to a well-thumbed Boswell, and to a garden where I shall mulch my rose-trees and watch the buds coming with as rich a satisfaction as any that the hot battle of the day has given me. But there is another thing I shall ask for. On the lower shelf of the bookcase, close to the Boswell, there will have to be a box of chessmen and a chessboard, and the men who were boys when I was a boy, and who come and sit with me, will be expected after supper to set out the chessmen as instinctively as they fill their pipes. And then for an hour, or it may be two, we shall enter into that rapturous realm where the knight prances and the bishop lurks with his shining sword and the rooks come crashing through in double file. The fire will sink and we shall not stir it, the clock will strike and we shall not hear it, the pipe will grow cold and we shall forget to relight it.

Blessed be the memory of him who gave the world this immortal game. For the price of a taxicab ride or a visit to the cinema, you may, thanks to that unknown benefactor, possess a world of illimitable adventures. When Alice passed through the Looking Glass into Wonderland, she did not more completely leave the common day behind than when you sit down before the chessboard with a stout foe before you and pass out into this magic realm of bloodless combat. I have heard unhappy people say that it is "dull." Dull, my dear sir or madam? Why, there is no excitement on this earth comparable with this kingly game. I have had moments at Lord's, I admit, and at the Oval. But here is a game which is all such moments, where you are up to the eyes in plots and ambuscades all the time, and the fellow in front of you is up to his eyes in them, too. What agonies as you watch his glance wandering over the board. Does he suspect that trap? Does he see the full meaning of that offer of the knight which seems so tempting?... His hand touches the wrong piece and your heart thumps a Te Deum. Is he?... yes ... no ... he pauses ... he removes his hand from the piece ... oh, heavens, his eye is wandering back to that critical pawn ... ah, light is dawning on him ... you see it illuminating his face as he bends over the board, you hear a murmur of revelation issuing from his lips ... he is drawing back from the precipice ... your ambuscade is in vain and now you must start plotting and scheming all over again.

Nay, say it is anything you like, but do not say it is dull. And do not, please, suggest that I am talking of it as an old man's game only. I have played it since I was a boy, forty years ago, and I cannot say at what age I have loved it best. It is a game for all ages, all seasons, all sexes, all climates, for summer evenings or winter nights, for land or for sea. It is the very water of Lethe for sorrow or disappointment, for there is no oblivion so profound as that which it offers for your solace. And what satisfaction is there comparable with a well-won "mate"? It is different from any other joy that games have to offer. There is a swift delight in a late "cut" or a ball that spread-eagles the other fellow's wicket; there is a delicate pleasure in a long jenny neatly negotiated, in a drive that sails straight from the tee towards the flag on the green, in a hard return that hits the back line of the tennis court. But a perfect "mate" irradiates the mind with the calm of indisputable things. It has the absoluteness of mathematics, and it gives you victory ennobled by the sense of intellectual struggle and stern justice. There are "mates" that linger in the memory like a sonnet of Keats.

It is medicine for the sick mind or the anxious spirit. We need a means of escape from the infinite, from the maze of this incalculable life, from the burden and the mystery of a world where all things "go contrary," as Mrs. Gummidge used to say. Some people find the escape in novels that move faithfully to that happy ending which the tangled skein of life denies us. Some find it in hobbies where the mind is at peace in watching processes that are controllable and results that with patience are assured. But in the midst of this infinity I know no finite world so complete and satisfying as that I enter when I take down the chessmen and marshal my knights and squires on the chequered field. It is then I am truly happy. I have closed the door on the infinite and inexplicable and have come into a kingdom where justice reigns, where cause and effect follow "as the night the day," and where, come victory or come defeat, the sky is always clear and the joy unsullied.

ON THE DOWNS

We spread our lunch on the crown of one of those great billows of the downs that stand along the sea. Down in the hollows tiny villages or farmsteads stood in the midst of clumps of trees, and the cultivated lands looked like squares of many-coloured carpets, brown carpets and yellow carpets and green carpets, with the cloud shadows passing over them and moving like battalions up the gracious slopes of the downs beyond. A gleam of white in the midst of one of the brown fields caught the eye. It seemed like a patch of snow that had survived the rigours of the English summer, but suddenly it rose as if blown by the wind and came towards us in tiny flakes of white that turned to seagulls. They sailed high above us uttering that querulous cry that seems to have in it all the unsatisfied hunger of the sea.

In this splendid spaciousness the familiar forms seem incredibly diminutive. That little speck moving across one of the brown carpets is a ploughman and his team. That white stream that looks like milk flowing over the green carpet is a flock of sheep running before the sheep-dog to another pasture. And the ear no less than the eye learns to translate the faint suggestions into known terms. At first it seems that, save for the larks that spring up here and there with their cascades of song, the whole of this immense vacancy is soundless. But listen. There is "the wind on the heath, brother." And below that, and only audible when you have attuned your ear to the silence, is the low murmur of the sea.

You begin to grow interested in probing the secrecies of this great stillness. That? Ah, that was the rumble of some distant railway train going to Brighton or Eastbourne. But what was that? Through the voices of the wind and the sea that we have learned to distinguish we catch another sound, curiously hollow and infinitely remote, not vaguely pervasive like the murmur of the sea, but round and precise like the beating of a drum somewhere on the confines of the earth.

"The guns!"

Yes, the guns. Across fifty miles of sea and fifty miles of land the sound is borne to us as we sit in the midst of this great peace of earth and sky. When once detached, as it were, from the vague murmurs of the breathing air it becomes curiously insistent. It throbs on the ear almost like the beating of a pulse—baleful, sepulchral, like the strokes of doom. We begin counting them, wondering whether they are the guns of the enemy or our own, speculating as to the course of the battle.

We have become spectators of the great tragedy, and the throb of the guns touches the scene with new suggestions. Those cloud shadows drifting across the valley and up the slopes of the downs on the other side take on the shapes of massed battalions. The apparent solitude does not destroy the impression. There is no solitude so complete to the outward eye as that which broods over the country when the armies face each other in the grips of death. I have looked from the mountain of Rheims across just such a valley as this. Twenty miles of battle front lay before me, and in all that great field of vision there was not a moving thing visible. There were no cattle in the fields and no ploughmen following their teams. Roads marched across the landscape, but they were empty roads. It was as though life had vanished from the earth. Yet I knew that all over that great valley the earth was crawling with life and full of immense and sinister secrecies—the galleries of the sappers, the trenches and redoubts, the hiding-places of great guns, the concealed observations of the watchers. Yes, it was just such a scene as this. The only difference was that you had not to put your ear to the ground to catch the thunder of the guns.

But the voice of war that has broken in upon our peace fades when we are once more on the move over the downs, and the visions it has brought with it seem unreal and phantasmal in their serene and sunlit world. The shadows turn to mere shadows again, and we tread the wild thyme and watch the spiral of the lark with careless rapture. We dip down into a valley to a village hidden among the trees, without fear or thought of bomb-proof shelters and masked batteries, and there in a cottage with the roses over the porch we take rest and counsel over the teacups. Then once more on to the downs. The evening shadows are stretching across the valleys, but on these spacious heights the sunshine still rests. Some one starts singing that jolly old song, "The Farmer's Boy," and soon the air resounds to the chorus:

"To plough and sow, to reap and mow,
And be a farmer's boy-o-o-o-oy,
And be a farmer's boy."

No one recalls the throbbing of the guns or stops to catch it from amidst the murmurs of the air. This—this is the reality. That was only an echo from a bad dream from which we have awakened.

And when an hour or two later we reach the little village by the sea we rush for the letters that await us with eager curiosity. There is silence in the room as each of us devours the budget of news awaiting us. I am vaguely conscious as I read that some one has left the room with a sense of haste. I go up to my bedroom, and when I return the sitting-room is empty save for one figure. I see at a glance that something has happened.

"Robert has been killed in battle," he says. How near the sound of the guns had come!

ON SHORT LEGS AND LONG LEGS

A day or two ago a soldier, returned from the front, was loudly inveighing in a railway carriage against the bumptiousness and harshness of the captain under whom he had served. "Let me git 'im over 'ere," he said, "and I'll lay 'im out–see if I don't. I've 'ad enough of 'is bullyin'. It ain't even as if 'e was a decent figure of a man. 'E don't stand more'n five-feet-two. I could knock 'im out with one 'and, and I'd 'ave done it before now only you mustn't out there. If you did you'd get a pound o' lead pumped into you."

Now, I dare say little five-feet-two deserved all that was said of him, and all he will get by way of punishment; but the point about the remark that interests me is the contempt it revealed for the man of small stature. There's no doubt that a little man starts with a grievance, with an aggravating sense of an inferiority that has nothing to do with his real merits. I know the feeling. For myself, I am just the right height–no more, no less. I am five-feet-nine-and-a-half, and I wouldn't be a shade different either way. I dare say that is the general experience. Everyone feels that his own is really the ideal standard. It is so in most things. Aristotle said that a man ought to marry at thirty-eight. I think he said it because he himself married at thirty-eight. Now, I married at twenty-three, and my opinion is that the right age at which to get married–if you are of the marrying sort–is twenty-three. In short, whatever we do or whatever we are, we have a deep-rooted conviction that we are "it." And it is well that it should be so. Without this innocent self-satisfaction there would be a lot more misery in the world.

But though I am the perfect height of five-feet-nine-and-a-half, I always feel depressed and out-classed in the presence of a man, say of six-feet-two. He may be an ass, but still I have to look up to him in a physical sense, and the mere act of looking up seems to endow him with a moral advantage. I feel a grievance at the outrageous length of the fellow, and find I want to make him fully understand that though I am only five-feet-nine-and-a-half in stature, my intellectual measurement is about ten feet, and that I am looking down on him much more than he is looking down on me.

It is this irksome self-consciousness that is the permanent affliction of the physically small man. Indeed, it is the affliction of anyone who has any physical peculiarity–a hare-lip, for example. Byron raged all his life against his club-foot, and doubtless that malformation was largely the cause of his savage contempt for a world that went about on two well-matched feet. I am sure that if I had a strawberry mark on the face I should never think about anything else. If I talked to anyone I should find him addressing his words to my strawberry mark. I should feel that he was deliberately and offensively dwelling on my disfigurement, saying to himself how glad he was he hadn't a strawberry mark and what a miserable chap I must be with such an article. He would not be doing anything of the sort, of course. He would probably be doing his best to keep his eyes off the strawberry mark. But I shouldn't think so, for I should be in that unhealthy condition of mind in which the whole world would seem to revolve around my strawberry mark.

And so with the small man. He lives in perpetual consciousness that the world is talking over his head, not because there is less sense in his head than in other heads, but simply because his legs are shorter than the popular size of legs. He is either overlooked altogether, or he is looked down upon, and in either case he is miserable. Occasionally his shortage lays him open to public ridicule. A barrister whom I knew—a man with a large head, a fair-sized body, and legs not worth mentioning—once rose to address a judge before whom he had not hitherto appeared. He had hardly opened his mouth when the judge remarked severely: "It is usual for counsel to stand in addressing the Court." "My lord," said the barrister, "I am standing."

Now can you imagine an agony more bitter than that to a sensitive man? I daresay he lost his case, for he must certainly have lost his head. You cannot cross-examine a witness effectively when you are thinking all the time about your miserable legs. And even if he won his case it probably gave him no comfort, for he would feel that the jury had given their verdict out of pity for the "little 'un." It is this self-consciousness that is the cause of that assertiveness and vanity that are often characteristic of the little man. He is probably not more assertive or more vain than the general run of us, but we can keep those defects dark, so to speak. He, on the other hand, has to go through life on tip-toe, carrying his head as high as his neck will lift it, and saying, as it were: "Hi! you long-legged fellows, don't forget me!" And this very reasonable anxiety to have "a place in the sun" gives him the appearance of being aggressive and vain. He is only trying to get level with the long-legged people, just as the short-sighted man tries to get level with the long-sighted man by wearing spectacles.

The discomfort of the very tall man is less humiliating than that of the small man, but it is also very real. He is just as much removed from contact with the normal world, and he has the added disadvantage of being horribly conspicuous. He can never forget himself, for all heads look up at him as he passes. He doesn't fit any doorway; he can't buy ready-made clothes; if he sleeps in a strange bed he has to leave his feet outside; and in the railway carriage or a bus he has to tie his legs into uncomfortable knots to keep them out of the way. In short, he finds himself a nuisance in a world made for people of five-feet-nine-and-a-half. But he has one advantage over the small man. He does not have to ask for notice. The result is that while the little man often seems vain and pushful, the giant usually is very tame, and modest, and unobtrusive. The little man wants to be seen: the giant wants not to be seen.

And so it comes about that our virtues and our failings have more to do with the length of our legs than we think.

ON A PAINTED FACE

The other day I met in the street a young lady who, but yesterday, seemed to me a young girl. She had in the interval taken that sudden leap from youth to maturity which is always so wonderful and perplexing. When I had seen her last there would have been no impropriety in giving her a kiss in the street. Now I should as little have thought of offering to kiss her as of whistling to the Archbishop of Canterbury if I had seen that dignitary passing on the other side of the road. She had taken wing and flown from the nest. She was no longer a child: she was a personage. I found myself trying (a little clumsily) to adapt my conversation to her new status, and when I left her I raised my hat a trifle more elaborately than is my custom.

But the thing that struck me most about her, and the thing that has set me writing about her, was this: I noticed that her face was painted and powdered. Now if there is one thing I abominate above all others it is a painted face. On the stage, of course, it is right and proper. The stage is a world of make-believe, and it is the business of the lady of sixty to give you the impression that she is a sweet young thing of seventeen. There is no affectation in this. It is her vocation to be young, and she follows it as willingly or unwillingly as you or I follow our respective callings. At the moment, for example, I would do anything to escape writing this article, for the sun is shining in the bluest of April skies and the bees are foraging in the orchard, and everything calls me outside to the woods and hills. But I must bake my tale of bricks first with as much pretence of enjoying the job as possible. And in the same way, and perhaps sometimes with the same distaste, the Juliet of middle age puts on the bloom of the Juliet of seventeen.

But that any one, not compelled to do it for a living, should paint the face or dye the hair is to me unintelligible. It is like attempting to pass off a counterfeit coin. It is either a confession that one is so ashamed of one's face that one dare not let it be seen in public, or it is an attempt to deceive the world into accepting you as something other than you are. It has the same effect on the observer that those sham oak beams and uprights that are so popular on the front of suburban houses have. They are not real beams or uprights. They do not support anything, or fill any useful function. They are only a thin veneer of oak stuck on to pretend that they are the real thing. They are a detestable pretence, and I would rather live in a hovel than in a house tricked out with such vulgar deceits that do not deceive.

And in the same way the paint on the face and the dye on the hair never really achieve their object. If they did they would not cease to be a sham, but at least they would not be a transparent sham. There are, of course, degrees of failure. Mrs. Gamp's curls were so obviously false that they could not be said to be intended to deceive. On the other hand, the great lady who employs the most scientific face-makers in order to defeat the encroachments of Time does very nearly succeed. But her failure is really more tragic than that of Mrs. Gamp. How tragic I realised one day when I was introduced to a distinguished "society" woman, whose youthful beauty was popularly supposed to have survived to old age. At a distance she did indeed seem to be a miracle of girlish loveliness. But when I came close to her and saw the old, bleared eyes in the midst of that beautifully enamelled face, the shock had in it something akin to horror. It was as though Death himself was peeping out triumphantly through the painted mask. And in that moment I seemed to see all the pitiful years of struggle that this unhappy woman had devoted to the pretence of never growing older. Her pink and white cheeks were not a thing of beauty. They were only a grim jest on herself, on her ambitions, her ideals, her poor little soul.

Why should we be so much afraid of wrinkles and grey hairs? In their place they can be as beautiful as the freshest glow on the face of youth. There is a beauty of the sunrise and a beauty of the sunset. And of the two the beauty of the sunset is the deeper and more spiritual. There are some faces that seem to grow in loveliness as the snows fall around them, and the acid of Time bites the gracious lines deeper. The dimple has become a crease, but it is none the less beautiful, for in that crease is the epic of a lifetime. To smooth out the crease, to cover it with the false hue of youth, is to turn the epic into a satire.

And if the painted face of age is horrible the painted face of youth is disgusting. It is artistically bad and spiritually worse. It is the mark of a debased taste and a shallow mind. It is like painting the lily or adding a perfume to the violet, and has on one the unpleasant effect that is made by the heavy odours in which the same type of person drenches herself, so that to pass her is like passing through a sickly fog. These things are the symptom of a diseased mind—a mind that has lost the healthy love of truth and nature, and has taken refuge in falsities and shams. The paint on the face does not stop at the cheeks. It stains the soul.

ON WRITING AN ARTICLE

I was putting on my boots just now in what the novelists call "a brown study." There was no urgent reason for putting on my boots. I was not going out, and my slippers were much more comfortable. But something had to be done. I wanted a subject for an article. Now if you are accustomed to writing articles for a living, you will know that sometimes the difficulty is not writing the article, but choosing a subject. It is not that subjects are few: it is that they are so many. It is not poverty you suffer from, but an embarrassment of riches. You are like Buridan's ass. That wretched creature starved between two bundles of hay, because he could not make up his mind which bundle to turn to first. And in that he was not unlike many human beings. There was an eighteenth-century statesman, for example, who used to find it so difficult to make a choice that he would stand at his door looking up the street and down the street, and finally go inside again, because he couldn't decide whether to go up or down. He would stay indoors all the morning considering whether he should ride out or walk out, and he would spend all the afternoon regretting that he had done neither one nor the other.

I have always had a great deal of sympathy with that personage, for I share his temperamental indecision. I hate making up my mind. If I go into a shop to choose a pair of trousers my infirmity of purpose grows with every new sample that is shown me, and finally I choose the wrong thing in a fit of desperation. If the question is a place for a holiday, all the artifices of my family cannot extract from me a decided preference for any place in particular. Bournemouth? Certainly. How jolly that walk along the sands by Poole Harbour to Studland and over the hills to Swanage. But think of the Lake District ... and North Wales ... and Devon ... and Cornwall ... and ... I do not so much make decisions as drift into them or fall into them. I am what you might call an Eleventh Hour Man. I take a header just as the clock is about to strike for the last time.

This common failing of indecision is not necessarily due to intellectual laziness. It may be due, as in the case of Goschen, to too clear a vision of all the aspects of a subject. "Goschen," said a famous First Sea Lord, "was the cleverest man we ever had at the Admiralty, and the worst administrator. He saw so many sides to a question that we could never get anything done." A sense of responsibility, too, is a severe check on action. I doubt whether anyone who has dealt with affairs ever made up his mind with more painful questionings than Lord Morley. I have heard him say how burdensome he found the India Office, because day by day he had to make irrevocable decisions. A certain adventurous recklessness is necessary for the man of affairs. Joseph Chamberlain had that quality. Mr. Churchill has it to-day. If it is controlled by high motives and a wide vision it is an incomparable gift. If it is a mere passion for having one's own way it is only the gift of the gambler.

But, you ask, what has this to do with putting on my boots? It is a reasonable question. I will tell you. For an hour I had paced my room in my slippers in search of a subject. I had looked out of the window over the sunlit valley, watched the smoke of a distant train vanishing towards the west, observed the activities of the rooks in a neighbouring elm. I had pared my nails several times with absent-minded industry, and sharpened every pencil I had on me with elaborate care. But the more I pared my nails and the more I sharpened my pencils the more perplexed I grew as to the theme for an article. Subjects crowded on me, "not single spies, but in battalions." They jostled each other for preference, they clamoured for notice as I have seen the dock labourers clamouring for a job at the London docks. They held out their hands and cried, "Here am I: take me." And, distracted by their importunities and starving in the midst of plenty, I fished in my pocket for a pencil I had not sharpened. There wasn't one left.

It was at this moment that I remembered my boots. Yes, I would certainly put on my boots. There was nothing like putting on one's boots for helping one to make up one's mind. The act of stooping changed the current of the blood. You saw things in a new light—like the man who looked between his legs at Bolton Abbey, and cried to his friend: "Oh, look this way; it's extraordinary what a fresh view you get." So I fetched my boots and sat down to put them on.

The thing worked like a charm. For in my preoccupied condition I picked up my right boot first. Then mechanically I put it down and seized the left boot. "Now why," said I, "did I do that?" And then the fact flashed on me that all my life I had been putting on my left boot first. If you had asked me five minutes before which boot I put on first, I should have said that there was no first about it; yet now I found I was in the grip of a habit so fixed that the attempt to put on my right boot first affected me like the scraping of a harsh pencil on a slate. The thing couldn't be done. The whole rhythm of habit would be put out of joint. I became interested. How, I wondered, do I put on my jacket? I rose, took it off, found that my right arm slipped automatically into its sleeve, tried the reverse process, discovered that it was as difficult as an unfamiliar gymnastic operation. Why, said I, I am a mere bundle of little habits of which I am unconscious. This thing must be looked into. And then came into my mind that fascinating book of Samuel Butler's on *Life and Habit*. Yes, certainly, here was a subject that would "go." I dismissed all the importunate beggars who had been clamouring in my mind, took out a pencil, seized a writing pad, and sat down to write on "The Force of Habit."

And here I am. I have got to the end of my article without reaching my subject. I have looked up and down the street so long that it is time to go indoors.

ON A CITY THAT WAS

I saw in a newspaper a few days ago some pictures of the ruins of the Cloth Hall and the Cathedral at Ypres. They were excellent photographs, but the impression they left on my mind was of the futility even of photography to convey any real sense of that astonishing scene of desolation which was once the beautiful city of Ypres. We talk of Ypres as if it were still a city in being, in which men trade, and children play, and women go about their household duties. In a vague way we feel that it is so. In a vague way I felt that it was so myself until I entered it and found myself in the presence of the ghost of a city.

How wonderful is the solitude and the silence in the midst of which it stands like the ruin of some ancient and forgotten civilisation. Far behind you have left the hurry and tumult of the great armies—every village seething with a strange and tumultuous life, soldiers bargaining with the women for potatoes and cabbages in the marketplace, boiling their pots in the fields, playing football by the way side, mending the roads, marching, camping, feeding, sleeping; officers flying along the roads on horseback or in motorcars, vast processions of lorries coiling their way over the landscape, or standing at rest with their death-dealing burdens while the men take their mid-day meal; giant "caterpillars" dragging great guns along the highway. Everywhere the sense of a fearful urgency, everywhere the feeling of a brooding and awful presence that overshadows the heavens with a cosmic menace. It is as though you are living on the slopes of some vast volcano whose eruptions may at any moment submerge all this phantasmal life in a sea of molten lava. And, hark! through the sounds of the roads and the streets, the chaffering of the market-place, the rush of motor-cars, the rhythmic tramp of men, there comes a dull, hollow roar, as from the mouth of a volcano itself.

As you advance the scene changes. The movement becomes more feverish, more intense. The very breath of the volcano seems to fan your cheek, and the hollow roar has become near and plangent. It is no longer like the breaking of great seas on a distant shore: it is like thunder rending the sky above you. A little further, and another subtle change is observable. On either hand the land has become solitary and unkempt. All the life of the fields has vanished and the soldiers are in undisputed possession. Then even the soldiers seem left behind, and you enter the strange solitude where the war is waged. Before you rises the great mound of Ypres. In the distance it looks like a living city with quaintly broken skyline, but as you approach you see that it is only the tomb of a city standing there desolate and shattered in the midst of a universal desolation.

It is midday as you pass through its streets, but there is no moving thing visible amidst the ruins. The very spirit of loneliness is about you—not the invigorating loneliness of the mountain tops, but the sad loneliness of the grave. I have stood upon the ruins of Carthage, but even there I did not feel the same sense of solitude that I felt as I walked the streets of Ypres. There, at least, the birds were singing above you, and the Arab sat beside his camel on the grass in the sunshine. Here nature itself seems blasted by some dreadful flame of death. The streets preserve their contours, but on either side the houses stand like gaunt skeletons, roofless and shattered, fronts knocked out, floors smashed through or hanging in fragments, bedsteads tumbling down through the broken ceiling of the sitting-room, pictures askew on the tottering walls, household treasures a forlorn wreckage, hats still hanging on the hat-pegs, the table-cloth still laid, the fireplace lustreless with the ashes of the last fire.

And in the centre of this scene of utter misery the Cathedral and the Cloth Hall, still towering above the general desolation, sublime even in their ruin, the roofs gone, the interiors a heap of rubbish—the rubbish of priceless things—the outer walls battered and broken, but standing as they have stood for centuries. Most wonderful of all, as I saw it, a single pinnacle of the Cloth Hall still standing above the wreck, slender and exquisitely carven, pointing like an accusing finger to the eternal tribunal. For long the Germans had been shelling that Finger of Ypres. They shelled it the afternoon I was there and filled the market-place with great masses of masonry from the walls. But they shelled it in vain, and as I left Ypres in the twilight, when the thunder of the guns had ceased, and looked back on the great mound of "the city that was," I saw above the ruins the finger still pointing heavenward.

But if the solitude of Ypres is memorable, the silence is terrible. It is the silence of imminent and breathless things, full of strange secrets, thrilling with a fearful expectation, broken by sudden and shattering voices that speak and then are still—voices that seem to come out of the bowels of the earth near at hand and are answered by voices more distant, the vicious hiss of the shrapnel, the crisp rattle of the machine-guns, the roar of "Mother," that sounds like an invisible express train thundering through the sky above you. The solitude and the silence assume an oppressive significance. They are only the garment of the mighty mystery that envelops you. You feel that these dead walls have ears, eyes, and most potent voices, that you are not in the midst of a great loneliness, but that all around the earth is full of most tremendous secrets. And then you realise that the city that is as dead as Nineveh to the outward eye is the most vital city in the world.

One day it will rise from its ashes, its streets will resound once more with jest and laughter, its fires will be relit, and its chimneys will send forth the cheerful smoke. But its glory throughout all the ages will be the memory of the days when it stood a mound of ruins on the plain with its finger pointing in mute appeal to heaven against the infamies of men.

ON PLEASANT SOUNDS

The wind had dropped, and on the hillside one seemed to be in a vast and soundless universe. Far down in the valley a few lights glimmered in the general darkness, but apart from these one might have fancied oneself alone in all the world. Then from some remote farmstead there came the sound of a dog barking. It rang through the night like the distant shout of a friend. It seemed to fill the whole arch of heaven with its reverberations and to flood the valley with the sense of companionship. It brought me news from the farm. The day's tasks were over, the cattle were settled for the night, the household were at their evening meal, and the watch-dog had resumed his nocturnal charge. His bark seemed to have in it the music of immemorial things—of labour and rest, and all the cheerful routine and comradeship of the fields.

It is only in the country that one enjoys the poetry of natural sounds. A dog barking in a suburban street is merely a disturber of the peace, and I know of nothing more forlorn than the singing of a caged bird in, let us say, Tottenham Court Road. Wordsworth's Poor Susan found a note of enchantment in the song of the thrush that sang at the corner of Wood Street, off Cheapside. But it was only an enchantment that passed into deeper sadness as the vision of the green pastures which it summoned up faded into the drab reality:

> ... they fade,
> The mist and the river, the hill and the shade:
> The stream will not flow and the hill will not rise,
> And the colours have passed away from her eyes.

There is something in the life of towns which seems to make the voices of the country alien and sorrowful. They are lost in the tumult, and, if heard, sound only like a reproach against a fretful world, an echo from some Eden from which we have been exiled.

In the large silence of the countryside sounds have a significance and intimacy that they cannot have where life is crowded with activities and interests. In a certain sense life here is richer because of its poverty—because of its freedom from the thousand distractions that exhaust its emotion and scatter its energies. Because we have little we discover much in that little.

Take the sound of church bells. In the city it is hardly more pleasing than the song of the bird in Tottenham Court Road. It does not raise my spirits, it only depresses them. But when I heard the sound of the bells come up from the valley last evening, it seemed like the bringer of a personal message of good tidings. It had in it the rapture of a thousand memories—memories of summer eves and snowy landscapes, of vanished faces and forgotten scenes. It was at once stimulating and calming, and spoke somehow the language of enduring and incommunicable things.

It is, I suppose, the associations of sounds rather than their actual quality which make them pleasant or unpleasant. The twitter of sparrows is, in itself, as prosaic a sound as there is in nature, but I never hear it on waking without a feeling of inward peace. It seems to link me with some incredibly remote and golden morning, and with a child in a cradle waking for the first time to light and sound and consciousness.

And so with that engaging ruffian of the feathered world, the rook. It has no more music in its voice than a tin kettle; but what jollier sound is there on a late February morning than the splendid hubbub of a rookery when the slovenly nests are being built in the naked and swaying branches of the elms? Betsy Trotwood was angry with David Copperfield's father because he called his house Blunderstone Rookery. "Rookery, indeed!" she said. It is almost the only point of disagreement I have with that admirable woman. Not to love a rookery is *prima facie* evidence against you. I have heard of men who have bought estates because of the rookery, and I have loved them for their beautiful extravagance. I am sure I should have liked David Copperfield's father from that solitary incident recorded of him. He was not a very practical or business-like man, I fear; but people who love rookeries rarely are. You cannot expect both the prose and the poetry of life for your endowment.

How much the feeling created by sound depends upon the setting may be illustrated by the bagpipes. The bagpipes in a London street is a thing for ribald laughter, but the bagpipes in a Highland glen is a thing to stir the blood, and make the mind thrill to memories of

> Old, unhappy, far off things.
> And battles long ago.

It is so even with the humble concertina. That instrument is to me the last expression of musical depravity. It is the torture which Dante would provide for me in the last circle of Hell. But the sound of a concertina on a country road on a dark night is as cheerful a noise as I want to hear. But just as Omar loved the sound of a *distant* drum, so distance is an essential part of the enchantment of my concertina.

And of all pleasant sounds what is there to excel the music of the hammer and the anvil in the smithy at the entrance to the village? No wonder the children love to stand at the open door and see the burning sparks that fly and hear the bellows roar. I would stand at the open door myself if I had the pluck, for I am as much a child as any one when the hammer and the anvil are playing their primeval music. It is the oldest song of humanity played with the most ancient instruments. Here we are at the very beginning of our story—here we stand in the very dawn of things. What lineage so noble as that of the smith? What task so ancient and so honourable? With such tools the first smith smote music out of labour, and began the conquest of things to the accompaniment of joyous sounds. In those sounds I seem to hear the whole burden of the ages.

I think I will take another stroll down to the village. It will take me past the smithy.

ON SLACKENING THE BOW

I was in a company the other evening in which the talk turned upon the familiar theme of the Government and its fitness for the job in hand. The principal assailant was what I should call a strenuous person. He seemed to suggest that if the conduct of the war had been in the hands of earnest-minded persons—like himself, for example—the business would have been over long ago.

"What can you expect," he said, the veins at the side of his forehead swelling with strenuousness, "from men who only play at war? Why, I was told by a man who was dining with Asquith not long ago that he was talking all the time about Georgian poetry, and that apparently he knew more about the subject than anybody at the table. Fiddling while Rome is burning, I call it."

"Did you want him to hold a Cabinet Council over the dinner-table?" I asked. The strenuous person killed me with a look of scorn.

But all the same, so far from being shocked to learn that Mr. Asquith can talk about poetry in these days, the fact, if it be a fact, increases my confidence in his competence for his task. I should suffer no pain even if I heard that he took a hand of cards after dinner, and I hope he takes care to get a game of golf at the week-end. I like men who have great responsibilities to carry their burdens easily, and to relax the bow as often as possible. The bigger the job you have in hand the more necessary it is to cultivate the habit of detachment. You want to walk away from the subject sometimes, as the artist walks away from his canvas to get a better view of his work. I never feel sure of an article until I have put it away, forgotten it, and read it again with a fresh mind, disengaged from the subject and seeing it objectively rather than subjectively. It is the affliction of the journalist that he has to face the light before he has had time to withdraw to a critical distance and to see his work with the detachment of the public.

There is nothing more mistaken than the view that because a thing is serious you must be thinking about it seriously all the time. If you do that you cease to be the master of your subject: the subject becomes the master of you. That is what is the matter with the fanatic. He is so obsessed by his idea that he cannot relate it to other ideas, and loses all sense of proportion, and often all sense of sanity. I have seen more unrelieved seriousness in a lunatic asylum than anywhere else.

The key to success is to come to a task with a fresh mind. That was the meaning of the very immoral advice given by a don to a friend of mine on the day before an examination. "What would you advise me to read to-night?" asked my friend, anxious to make the most of the few remaining hours. "If I were you," said the don, "I shouldn't read anything. I should get drunk." He did not mean that the business was so unimportant that it did not matter what he did. He meant that it was so important that he must forget all about it, and come to it afresh from the outside. And he used the most violent illustration he could find to express his meaning.

It is with the mind as with the soil. If you want to get the best out of your land you must change the crops, and sometimes even let the land lie fallow. And if you want to get the best out of your mind on a given theme you must let it range and have plenty of diversion. And the more remote the diversion is from the theme the better. I know a very grave man whose days are spent in the most responsible work, who goes to see Charlie Chaplin once or twice every week, and laughs like a schoolboy all the time. I should not trust his work less on that account: I should trust it all the more. I should know that he did not allow it to get the whip hand of him, that he kept sane and healthy by running out to play, as it were, occasionally.

I think all solemn men ought to take sixpenny-worth of Charlie Chaplin occasionally. And I'm certain they ought to play more. I believe that the real disease of Germany is that it has never learned to play. The bow is stretched all the time, and the nation is afflicted with a dreadful seriousness that suggests the madhouse by its lack of humour and gaiety. The oppressiveness of life begins with the child. Germany is one of The two countries in the world where the suicide of children is a familiar social fact. Years ago when I was in Cologne I christened it the City of the Elderly Children, and no one, I think, can have had any experience of Germany without being struck by the premature gravity of the young. If Germany had had fewer professors and a decent sprinkling of cricket and football grounds perhaps things might have been different. I don't generally agree with copybook maxims, but all work and no play does make Jack (or, rather, Hans) a dull boy.

Perhaps it is true that we play too much; but I'm quite sure that the Germans have played too little, and if there must be a mistake on one side or the other, let it be on the side of too much play.

ON THE INTELLIGENT GOLF BALL

I read the other day an article by my colleague "Arcturus" which I thought was a little boastful. It referred to a bull-dog. Now I cannot tell what there is about a bull-dog that makes people haughty, but it is certain that I have never known a case in which the companionship of that animal has not had this effect. The man who keeps a bull-dog becomes after a time only fit for the company of a bull-dog. He catches the august pride of the animal, seems to think like a bulldog, to talk in the brief, scornful tones of a bulldog, and even to look fat and formidable like a bull-dog. That, however, is not an uncommon phenomenon among those who live with animals. Go to a fat stock show and look at the men around the cattle pens. Or recall the pork butchers you have known and tell me—. But possibly you, sir, who read these lines, are a pork butcher and resent the implication. Sir, your resentment is just. You are the exception, sir–a most notable exception.

But my object here is not merely to warn "Arcturus" of the perilous company he is keeping. I refer to his bull-dog panegyric also to justify me in enlarging on my own private vanity. If he is permitted to write to the extent of a column on a bull-dog, I can at least claim the same latitude in regard to a sensible subject like golf. And I have this advantage over him, that I have a real message. I have a hint to offer that will mean money in pocket to you.

And first let me say that I have nothing to teach you in the way of play. I am in that stage of the novitiate that seems sheer imbecility. When I get a good stroke I stare after it as stout Cortez stared at the Pacific, "with a wild surmise." But it is because I am a bad player that I feel I can be useful to you. For most of my time on the links is spent in looking for lost balls. Now, I do not object to looking for balls. I rather enjoy it. It is a healthy, open-air occupation that keeps the body exercised and the mind fallow. There are some people who think the spectacle of a grown-up man (with a family) looking in an open field for a ball that isn't there is ridiculous. They are mistaken. It is really, seen from the philosophic angle, a very noble spectacle. It is the symbol of deathless hope. It is part of the great discipline of the game. It is that part of the game at which I do best. There is not a spinney over the whole course that I do not know by heart. There is not a bit of gorse that I have not probed and been probed by. I must have spent hours in the ditches, and I have upon me the scars left by every hedgerow. And the result is that, while I am worthless as a golfer, I think I may claim to be quite in the first class at finding lost balls.

Now all discoveries hinge upon some sudden illumination. I had up to a certain point been a sad failure in recovering balls. I watched them fall with the utmost care and was so sure of them that I felt that I could walk blindfold and pick them up. But when I came to the spot the ball was not there. This experience became so common that at last the conclusion forced itself upon me that the golf ball had a sort of impish intelligence that could only be met by a superior cunning. I suspected that it deliberately hid itself, and that so long as it was aware that you were hunting for it, it took a fiendish delight in dodging you. If, said I, one could only let the thing suppose it was not being looked for it would be taken off its guard. I put the idea into operation, and I rejoice to say it works like a charm.

The method is quite simple. You lose the ball, of course, to begin with. That is easy enough. Then you search for it, and the longer you search the deeper grows the mystery of its vanishing. Your companions come and help you to poke the hedge and stir up the ditch, and you all agree that you have never known such a perfectly ridiculous thing before. And having clearly proved that the ball isn't anywhere in the neighbourhood, you take another out of the bag, and proceed with the game.

So far everything is quite ordinary. The game is over, the ball is lost, and you prepare to go. But you decide to go home by a rather roundabout way that brings you by the spot that you have scoured in vain. You are not going to search for the ball. That would simply put the creature up to some new artifice. No, you are just walking round that way accidentally. What so natural as that you should have your eyes on the ground? And there, sure enough, lies the ball, taken completely unaware. It is so ridiculously obvious that to say that it was lying there when you were looking for it so industriously is absurd. It simply couldn't have been there. You suspect that if after your search, instead of going on with the play you had hidden behind the hedge and watched, you would have seen the creature come out from its hole.

I do not expect to have my theory that the golf-ball has an intelligence accepted. The mystery is explicable, I am told, on the doctrine of the "fresh eye." You look for a thing so hard that you seem to lose the faculty of vision. Then you forget all about it and find it. The experience applies to all the operations of the mind. If I get "stuck" in writing an article I go and do a bit of physical work, ride a bicycle or merely walk round the garden, and the current flows again. Or you have a knotty problem to decide. You think furiously about it all day and get more hopelessly undecided the longer you think. Then you go to bed, and you wake in the morning with your mind made up. Hence the phrase, "I will sleep on it." It is this freshness of the vision, this faculty of passive illumination, that Wordsworth had in mind when he wrote:

> Think you, 'mid all this mighty sum
> Of things for ever speaking,
> That nothing of itself will come,
> But we must still be seeking?

And yet I cannot quite get rid of my fancy that the golf ball does enjoy the game.

ON A PRISONER OF WAR

There are still a few apples on the topmost branches of the trees in the orchard. They are there because David, the labourer, who used to come and lend us a hand in his odd hours—chiefly when the moon was up—is no longer available. You may remember how David opened his heart to me about enlisting when he stood on the ladder picking the pears last year. He did not like to go and he did not like to stay. All the other chaps had gone, and he didn't feel comfortable like in being left behind, but there was his mother and his wife and his Aunt Jane, and not a man to do a hand's turn for 'em or to dig their gardens if he went. And there was the allotment—that 'ud run to weeds. And ...

Well, the allotment has run to weeds. I passed it to-day and looked over the hedge and saw the chickweed and the thistles in undisputed possession. For David has gone. "It will take a long time to turn him into a soldier," we said when we saw him leave his thatched roof last spring to join up, and watched him shambling down the lane to the valley and the distant station. "The war will be over before he gets into the trenches," I said cheerfully to his wife, his mother, and Aunt Jane as they sat later in the day mingling their tears in the "parlour"—that apartment sacred to Sundays, funerals, and weddings. "Poor boy, what'll he do without his comfortable bed?" moaned his mother.

But by May there came news that David was in France. By June he was in the trenches, and woe sat heavy on the three women to whom the world without David was an empty place.

Then came silence. The postman comes up the lane on his bicycle to our straggling hamlet on the hillside twice a day, and after David had gone his visits to the cottages of the three women had been frequent. Sometimes he put his bicycle at the mother's gate, sometimes at David's gate, less often at Aunt Jane's gate. For David was an industrious correspondent, even though his letters were a laborious compromise between crosses and "hoping you are well as it leaves me at present."

But in August the postman ceased to call. Long before his hour you could see the three women watching for his coming. I think the postman got to dread turning the corner and facing the expectant women with empty hands. He could not help feeling that somehow he was to blame. At first he would stop and point out elaborately the reasons for delay in the post. Then, when this had become thin with time, he adopted the expedient of riding past the cottages very hard with eyes staring far ahead, as though he was going to a fire or was the bearer of an important dispatch.

But at the end of a fortnight or so he came round the corner one morning more in the old style. The women observed the change and went out to meet him. But their faces fell as they looked at the letter and saw that the handwriting was not David's. And the contents were as bad as they could be. The letter was from a lad in the valley who had "joined up" with David. He wrote from a hospital asking for news of his comrade, whom he had seen "knocked over" in the advance in which he himself had been wounded.

For the rest of the day, it was observed, the cottage doors were never opened. Nor did any one venture to break in on the misery of the women inside. The parson's wife came up in her gig from the valley, having heard the news, but she did not call. She only talked to the neighbours, who had had the details from the postman. Everyone felt the news like a personal blow, and even the widow Wigley, who lives down in the valley, was full of sympathy. She had never quite got over her resentment at the funeral of David's father. Her own husband had been carried to his grave on a hand-bier, but at the funeral of David's father there was a horse-drawn hearse and a carriage for the mourners. "They were always *such* people for show," said Mrs. Wigley. And the memory had rankled. But now it was buried.

Next day we saw the mother and the wife set out down the lane for the village post-office, and thereafter daily they went to await the arrival of letters, returning each day silent and hopeless. At last, in reply to inquiries which had been made at the War Office, there came the official statement that David had been reported "wounded and missing." We learned that this usually meant that the man was dead, but the women did not know this.

And, curiously enough, David's mother, who had been the most despairing of women, and seemed to regard David as dead even before he started, now discovered a genius for hopefulness. She had heard of a case from a neighbouring village of a man who had been reported dead, and who afterwards wrote from a prison camp in Germany, and she clung to this precedent with a confident tenacity that we did not try to weaken. It was foolish, of course, we said. She was pinning her faith to a case in a thousand; but the hope gave the women something to live for, and the wound would heal the better for the illusion.

And, after all, she was right. This morning we saw the postman call at the cottage. He handed a post card to the wife, and it was evident that something wonderful and radiant had happened. The women fell on each other "laughing happy." No more going into the house to shut the door on the world. They came out to share the great tidings with their neighbours. "David is alive! David is a prisoner in Germany.... He's wounded.... But he's going on all right.... He can't write yet.... But he will."

Yes, there was the post card all right. The English was not very good and the script was German, but the fact that David was alive in hospital shone clear and indisputable.

"It's as though he's raised from the dead," cried the wife through her tears.

The joy of the old mother was touched with solemnity. She is a great chapel-goer, and her utterance is naturally coloured by the Book with which she is most familiar.

"My son was dead, and is alive again," she said simply; "he was lost and is found."

When I went out into the orchard and saw the red-cheeked apples still clinging to the topmost branches I thought, "Perhaps David will be able to lend me a hand with those trees next autumn after all."

ON THE WORLD WE LIVE IN

In one of those charming articles which he writes in *The New Statesman*, Mr. J. Arthur Thomson tells of the wonderful world of odours to which we are largely strangers. No doubt in an earlier existence we relied much more upon our noses for our food, our safety, and all that concerned us, and had a highly developed faculty of smell which has become more or less atrophied.

Fee, fie, fo, fum,
I smell the blood of an Englishman,

said the Giant in the story. But that was long ago. If we were left to the testimony of our noses we could not tell an Englishman from a hippopotamus. To the bee, on the other hand, with its two or three thousand olfactory pores, the world is primarily a world of smell. If we could question that wonderful creature we should find that it thought and talked of nothing but the odours of the field. We should find that it had a range of experience in that realm beyond our wildest imaginings. We should find that there are more smells in heaven and earth than are dreamt of in our philosophy.

We talk of the world as if our sensations were the sum total of experience. But the truth is that there is an infinity of worlds outside our comprehension, worlds of vision and hearing and smell that are beyond our finite capacity, some so microscopic as to escape us at one end of the scale, some so vast and intangible as to escape us at the other end. I went into the garden just now to pick some strawberries. One of them tempted me forthwith by its ripe and luxuriant beauty. I bit into it and found it hollowed out in the centre, and in that luscious hollow was a colony of earwigs. For them that strawberry was the world, and a very jolly world too—abundance of food, a soft bed to lie on, and a chamber of exquisite perfumes. What, I wonder, was the thought of the little creatures as their comfortable world was suddenly shattered by some vast, inexplicable power beyond the scope of their vision and understanding? I could not help idly wondering whether the shell of our comfortable world has been broken by some power without which is as far beyond our apprehension as I was beyond the apprehension of the happy dwellers in the strawberry.

And it is not only the worlds which are peculiar to the myriad creatures of diverse instincts and faculties which are so strangely separate. We ourselves all dwell in worlds of infinite variety. I do not mean the social and professional worlds in which we move, though here, too, the world is not one but many. There is not much in common between the world as it appears to Sarah Ellen, who "runs" four looms in a Lancashire weaving shed during fifty-one weeks in the year, and my Lady Broadacres, who suns herself in Mayfair.

But I am speaking here of our individual world, the world of our private thought and emotions. My world is not your world, nor yours mine. We sit and talk with each other, we work together and play together, we exchange confidences and share our laughter and our experiences. But ultimately we can neither of us understand the world of the other—that world which is the sum of a million factors of unthinkable diversity, trifles light as air, memories, experiences, physical emotions, the play of light and colour and sound, attachments and antipathies often so obscure that we cannot even explain them to ourselves. We may feel a collective emotion under the impulse of some powerful event or personality. We may ebb and flow as a tide to the rhythm of a great melody or to the incantation of noble oratory. The news of a great victory in these days would move us to our common centre and bring all our separate worlds into a mighty chorus of thanksgiving. But even in these common emotions there are infinite shades of difference, and when they have passed we subside again into the world where we dwell alone.

Most of us are doomed to go through life without communicating the mysteries of our experience.

> Alas for those who never sing.
> But die with all their music in them.

It is the privilege of the artist in any medium to enrich the general life with the consciousness of the world that he alone has experienced. He gives us new kingdoms for our inheritance, makes us the sharers of his visions, opens out wider horizons, and floods our life with richer glories.

I entered such a kingdom the other afternoon. I turned out of the Strand, which was thronged and throbbing with the news of the great advance,—it was the first day of the battle of the Somme—and entered the Aldwych Theatre. As if by magic, I passed from the thrilling drama of the present into a realm

> Full of sweet dreams and health and quiet breathing—

into a sunlit world, where the zephyrs fan your cheek like a benediction and the brooks tinkle through the gracious landscape and melody is on every bough and joy and peace are all about you—the idyllic world where the marvellous child, Mozart, reigns like an enchanter. What though the tale of *The Magic Flute* is foolish beyond words. Who cares for the tale? Who thinks of the tale? It is only the wand in the hand of the magician. Though it be but a broomstick, it will open all the magic casements of earth and heaven, it will surround us with the choirs invisible, and send us forth into green pastures and by the cool water-brooks.

That was Mozart's vision of the world in his brief but immortal journey through it. Perhaps it was only a dream world, but what a dream to live through! And to him it was as real a world as that of Mr. Gradgrind, whose vision is shut in by what Burns called "the raised edge of a bawbee." We must not think that our world is the only one. There are worlds outside our experience. "Call that a sunset?" said the lady to Turner as she stood before the artist's picture. "I never saw a sunset like that." "No, madam," said Turner. "Don't you wish you had?" Perhaps your world and mine is only mean because we are near-sighted. Perhaps we miss the vision not because the vision is not there, but because we darken the windows with dirty hangings.

"I'M TELLING YOU"

The other day I went into the Law Courts to hear a case of some interest, and I soon became more interested in the counsel than in the case. They offered a curious contrast of method. One was emphatic and dogmatic. "I'm not asking you," he seemed to say to the judge and jury, "I'm telling you." The other was winning and conciliatory. He did not thrust his views down the jury's throats; he seemed to offer them for their consideration, and leave it at that. He was not there to dictate to them, but to hold his client's case up to the light, as it were, just as a draper holds a length of silk up before his customer. Now, as a matter of fact, I think the dogmatic gentleman had the better case and the stronger argument, but I noticed next day that the verdict went against him. He won his argument and lost his case.

That is what commonly happens with the dogmatic and argumentative man. He shuts up the mind to reason. He changes the ground from the issue itself to a matter of personal dignity. You are no longer concerned with whether the thing is right or wrong. You are concerned about showing your opponent that you are not to be bullied by him into believing what he wants you to believe. Even Johnson, who was, perhaps, the most dogmatic person that ever lived, knew that success in the argument was often fatal to success in the case. Dr. Taylor once commended a physician to him, and said: "I fight many battles for him, as many people in the country dislike him." "But you should consider, sir," replied Johnson, "that by every one of your victories he is a loser; for every man of whom you get the better will be very angry, and resolve not to employ him; whereas if people get the better of you in argument about him, they'll think, 'We'll send for Dr. —, nevertheless.'"

But Johnson fought not to convince, but for love of the argumentative victory. A great contemporary of his, whom he never met, and whom, if he had met, he would probably have insulted–Benjamin Franklin, to wit–preferred winning the case to winning the argument. While still a boy, he tells us, he was fascinated by the Socratic method, and instead of expressing opinions asked leading questions. He ceased to use words like "certainly," "undoubtedly," or anything that gave the air of positiveness to an opinion, and said "I apprehend," or "I conceive," a thing to be so and so.

"This habit," he says, "has been of great advantage to me when I have had occasion to inculcate my opinions and persuade men into measures that I have been engaged from time to time in promoting. And as the chief ends of conversation are to *inform* or to be *informed*, to *please* or to *persuade*, I wish well-meaning and sensible men would not lessen their power of doing good by a positive assuming manner, that seldom fails to disgust, tends to create opposition and to defeat most of those purposes for which speech was given us. In fact, if you wish to instruct others, a positive dogmatical manner in advancing your sentiments may occasion opposition and prevent a candid attention. If you desire instruction and improvement from others, you should not at the same time express yourself fixed in your present opinions. Modest and sensible men, who do not love disputation, will leave you undisturbed in the possession of your errors."

It is really, I suppose, our old friend "compulsion" again. We hate Prussianism in the realm of thought as much as in the realm of action. If I tell you you've got to believe so-and-so, your disposition is to refuse to do anything of the sort. It was the voluntary instinct that breathes in all of us that made Falstaff refuse to give Prince Hal reasons: "I give thee reasons? Though reasons were as plenty as blackberries I would not give thee reasons *on compulsion*—I."

I was once talking to a member of Parliament, who was lamenting that he had failed to win the ear of the House. He was puzzled by the failure. He was a fluent speaker; he knew his subject with great thoroughness, and his character was irreproachable; and yet when he rose the House went out. He was like a dinner-bell. He couldn't understand it. Yet everybody else understood it quite well. It was because he was always "telling you," and there is nothing the House of Commons dislikes so much as a schoolmaster. Probably the most successful speaker, judging by results, whoever rose in the House of Commons was Cobden. He was one of the few men in history who have changed a decision in Parliament by a speech. He did it because of his extraordinarily persuasive manner. He kept the minds of his hearers receptive and disengaged. He did not impress them with the fact that he was right and they were wrong. They forgot themselves when they saw the subject in a clear, white light, and were prepared to judge it on its merits rather than by their prejudices.

One of the few persuasive speakers I have heard in the House of Commons in recent years is Mr. Harold Cox. Many of his opinions I detest, but the engaging way in which he presents them makes you almost angry with yourself at disagreeing with him. You feel, indeed, that you must be wrong, and that such open-mindedness and such a friendly conciliatory manner as he shows must somehow be the evidence of a right view of things. As a matter of fact, of course, he is really a very dogmatic gentleman at the bottom—none more so. As indeed Franklin was. But he has the art to conceal the emphasis of his opinions, and so he makes even those who disagree with him listen to his case almost with a desire to endorse it.

It is a great gift. I wish I had got it.

ON COURAGE

I was asked the other day to send to a new magazine a statement as to the event of the war which had made the deepest impression on me. Without hesitation I selected the remarkable Christmas demonstrations in Flanders. Here were men who for weeks and months past had been engaged in the task of stalking each other and killing each other, and suddenly under the influence of a common memory, they repudiate the whole gospel of war and declare the gospel of brotherhood. Next day they began killing each other again as the obedient instruments of governments they do not control and of motives they do not understand. But the fact remains. It is a beam of light in the darkness, rich in meaning and hope.

But if I were asked to name the instance of individual action which had most impressed me I should find the task more difficult. Should I select something that shows how war depraves, or something that shows how it ennobles? If the latter I think I would choose that beautiful incident of the sailor on the *Formidable*.

He had won by ballot a place in one of the boats. The ship was going down, but he was to be saved. One pictures the scene: The boat is waiting to take him to the shore and safety. He looks at the old comrades who have lost in the ballot and who stand there doomed to death. He feels the passion for life surging within him. He sees the cold, dark sea waiting to engulf its victims. And in that great moment–the greatest moment that can come to any man–he makes the triumphant choice. He turns to one of his comrades. "You've got parents," he says. "I haven't." And with that word–so heroic in its simplicity–he makes the other take his place in the boat and signs his own death warrant.

I see him on the deck among his doomed fellows, watching the disappearing boat until the final plunge comes and all is over. The sea never took a braver man to its bosom. "Greater love hath no man than this ..."

Can you read that story without some tumult within you–without feeling that humanity itself is ennobled by this great act and that you are, in some mysterious way, better for the deed? That is the splendid fruit of all such sublime sacrifice. It enriches the whole human family. It makes us lift our heads with pride that we are men–that there is in us at our best this noble gift of valiant unselfishness, this glorious prodigality that spends life itself for something greater than life. If we had met this nameless sailor we should have found him perhaps a very ordinary man, with plenty of failings, doubtless, like the rest of us, and without any idea that he had in him the priceless jewel beside which crowns and coronets are empty baubles. He was something greater than he knew.

How many of us could pass such a test? What should I do? What would you do? We neither of us know, for we are as great a mystery to ourselves as we are to our neighbours. Bob Acres said he found that "a man may have a deal of valour in him without knowing it," and it is equally true that a man may be more chicken-hearted than he himself suspects. Only the occasion discovers of what stuff we are made—whether we are heroes or cowards, saints or sinners. A blustering manner will not reveal the one any more than a long face will reveal the other.

The merit of this sailor's heroism was that it was done with calculation—in cold blood, as it were, with that "two-o'clock-in-the-morning courage" of which Napoleon spoke as the real thing. Many of us could do brave things in hot blood, with a sudden rush of the spirit, who would fail if we had time, as this man had, to pause and think, to reckon, to doubt, to grow cold and selfish. The merit of his deed is that it was an act of physical courage based on the higher quality of moral courage.

Nor because a man fails in the great moment is he necessarily all a coward. Mark Twain was once talking to a friend of mine on the subject of courage in men, and spoke of a man whose name is associated with a book that has become a classic. "I knew him well," he said, "and I knew him as a brave man. Yet he once did the most cowardly thing I have ever heard of any man. He was in a shipwreck, and as the ship was going down he snatched a lifebelt from a woman passenger and put it on himself. He was saved, and she was drowned. And in spite of that frightful act I think he was not a coward. I know there was not a day of his life afterwards when he would not willingly and in cold blood have given his life to recall that shameful act."

In this case the failure was not in moral courage, but in physical courage. He was demoralised by the peril, and the physical coward came uppermost. If he had had time to recover his moral balance he would have died an honourable death. It is no uncommon thing for a man to have in him the elements both of the hero and the coward. You remember that delightful remark of Mrs. Disraeli, one of the most characteristic of the many quaint sayings attributed to that strange woman. "Dizzy," she said, "has wonderful moral courage, but no physical courage. I always have to pull the string of his shower bath." It is a capital illustration of that conflict of the coward and the brave man that takes place in most of us. Dizzy's moral courage carried him to the bath, but there his physical courage failed him. He could not pull the string that administered the cold shock. The bathroom is rich in such secrets, and life teems with them.

The true hero is he who unites the two qualities. The physical element is the more plentiful. For one man who will count the cost of sacrifice and, having counted it, pay the price with unfaltering heart, there are many who will answer the sudden call to meet peril with swift defiance. The courage that snatches a comrade from under the guns of the enemy or a child from the flames is, happily, not uncommon. It is inspired by an impulse that takes men out of themselves and by a certain spirit of challenge to fate that every one with a sporting instinct loves to take. But the act of the sailor of the *Formidable* was a much bigger thing. Here was no thrill of gallantry and no sporting risk. He dealt in cold certainties: the boat and safety; the ship and death; his life or the other's. And he thought of his comrade's old parents at home and chose death.

It was a great end. I wonder whether you or I would be capable of it. I would give much to feel that I could answer in the affirmative—that I could take my stand on the spiritual plane of that unknown sailor.

ON SPENDTHRIFTS

While everyone, I suppose, agrees that Lady Ida Sitwell richly deserves her three months' imprisonment, there are many who will have a sneaking pity for her. And that not because she is a woman of family who will suffer peculiar tortures from prison life. On the contrary, I have no doubt that a spell of imprisonment is just what she needs. In fact, it is what most of us need, especially most of those who live a life of luxurious idleness. To be compelled to get up early, to clean your cell, to wear plain clothes, to live on plain food, to observe regular hours, and do regular duties—this is no matter for tears, but for thankfulness. It is the sort of discipline that we ought to undergo periodically for our spiritual and even bodily health.

No, the sympathy that will be felt for Lady Ida is the sympathy which is commonly felt for the spendthrift—for the person who, no matter what his income, is congenitally incapable of making ends meet. The miser has no friends; but the spendthrift has generally too many. We avoid Harpagon as though he were a leper; but Falstaff, who, like Lady Ida, could "find no cure for this intolerable consumption of the purse," never lacked friends, and even Justice Shallow, it will be remembered, lent him a thousand crowns. There is no record of its having been repaid, though Falstaff was once surprised, in a moment of bitter humiliation, into admitting the debt. And Charles Surface and Micawber—who can deny them a certain affection? I have no doubt that Mrs. Micawber's papa, who "lived to bail Mr. Micawber out many times until he died lamented by a wide circle of friends," loved the fellow as you and I love him. I should deem it a privilege to bail out Micawber. But Elwes, the miser—ugh! the very name chills the blood.

The difference, I suppose, proceeds from the idea that while the miser is the soul of selfishness, the spendthrift is at bottom a good-natured fellow and a lover of his kind. No doubt the vice of the spendthrift has a touch of generosity, but it is often generosity at other people's expense, and is not seldom as essentially selfish as the vice of the miser. It is rather like the generosity of the man who, according to Sydney Smith, was so touched by a charity sermon that he picked his neighbour's pocket of a guinea and put it in the plate. I have no doubt that Lady Ida if she had got Miss Dobbs's money would have scattered it about with a very free hand, and would have contributed to the collection plate quite handsomely. But she was selfish none the less. It was her form of selfishness to enjoy the luxury of spending money she hadn't got, just as it was Elwes's form of selfishness to enjoy the luxury of saving money that he had got.

The point was very well stated by a famous miser whose son has since been in Parliament (I will not say on which side). The old man had accumulated a vast fortune, but, in the Scotch phrase, would have grudged you "the smoke off his porridge." (He died, by the way, properly enough, through walking home in the rain because he was too mean to take a cab.) He was once asked why he was so anxious to increase his riches, since his son would probably squander them, and he replied, "If my son gets as much pleasure out of squandering my money as I have had out of saving it, I shall not mind." Both the hoarding and the spending, you see, were in his view equally a matter of mere selfish pleasure.

But I admit that the uncalculating spirit that lands people in debt is a more engaging frailty than the calculating spirit of the miser. I know a delightful man who seems to have no more knowledge of the relation of income and expenditure than a kitten. If he gets £100 unexpectedly he does not look at it in relation to his whole needs. He does not remember rent, rates, taxes, baker, butcher, tailor. No. On the strength of it, he will order a new piano in the morning, buy his wife a sealskin jacket in the afternoon, and by the next day be deeper in the mire than ever, and wonder how he got there. And there is Jones's young wife, a charming woman, who is dragging her husband into debt with the same kittenish irresponsibility. She will leave Jones on the pavement with a remark that suggests that she is going into the shop to buy some pins, and will come out with a request for £10 for some "perfectly lovely" thing that has caught her eye. And Jones, being elderly, and still a little astonished at having won the affection of such a divinity, has not the courage to say "No."

To the people afflicted with these loose spending habits I would commend the lesson of a little incident I saw in a tram on the Embankment the other evening. There entered and sat beside me a working man, carrying his "kit" in a handkerchief, and wearing a scarf round his neck, a cloth cap, and corduroy trousers—obviously a labourer earning perhaps 25s. a week. He paid his fare, and then he took from his pocket a packet tied up in a handkerchief. He untied the knot, and there came forth a neat pocket-book with pencil attached. He opened it, and began to write. My curiosity was too much for my manners. Out of the tail of my eye I watched the motion of his fingers, and this is what he wrote: "Tram 1-1/2 d." In a flash I seemed to see the whole orderly life of that poor labourer. He had an anchorage in the tossing seas of this troublesome world. He had got hold of a lesson that Lady Ida Sitwell ought to try and learn during the next three months. It is this: Watch your spendings.

For it is the people who are more concerned about getting money than about how they spend it who come to grief. A very acute observer once told me that the principal difference between the Scotch people and the Lancashire people was that the former thought most about how they spent, and the latter most about how much they got. And the difference, he said, was the difference between a thrifty and an unthrifty people. I think that is true. Nothing is more common than to find people worse off as they get better off. They have learned the art of getting money and lost the art of spending it wisely. They pay their way on £200 a year and get hopelessly into debt on £500. They are safe in a rowing boat, but capsize in a sailing boat.

Here is an axiom which I offer to all spendthrifts: We cannot command our incomings; but we can control outgoings.

ON A TOP-HAT

A few days ago I went to a christening to make vows on behalf of the offspring of a gallant young officer now at the front. I conceived that the fitting thing on such an occasion was to wear a silk hat, and accordingly I took out the article, warmed it before the fire, and rubbed it with a hat pad until it was nice and shiny, put it on my head, and set out for the church. But I soon regretted the choice. It had no support from anyone else present, and when later I got out of the Tube and walked down the Strand I found that I was a conspicuous person, which, above all things, I hate to be. My hat, I saw, was observed. Eyes were turned towards me with that mild curiosity with which one remarks any innocent oddity or vanity of the streets.

I became self-conscious and looked around for companionship, but as my eye travelled along the crowded pavement I could see nothing but bowlers and trilbys and occasional straws. "Ah, here at last," said I, "is one coming." But a nearer view only completed my discomfiture, for it was one of those greasy-shiny hats which go with frayed trousers and broken boots, and which are the symbol of "better days," of hopes that are dead, and "drinks" that dally, of a social status that has gone and of a suburban villa that has shrunk to a cubicle in a Rowton lodging-house. I looked at greasy-hat and greasy-hat looked at me, and in that momentary glance of fellowship we agreed that we were "out of it."

I put my silk hat away at night with the firm resolution that nothing short of an invitation to Buckingham Palace, or some similar incredible disaster, should make me drag it into the light again. For the truth is that the war has given the top-hat a knock-out blow. It had been tottering on our brows for some time. There was a very hot summer a few years ago which began the revolution. The tyranny of the top-hat became intolerable, and quite "respectable" people began to be seen in the streets with Panamas and straws. But these were only concessions to an irresponsible climate, and the silk hat still held its ancient sway as the crown and glory of our City civilisation. And now it has toppled down and is on the way, perhaps, to becoming as much a thing of the past as wigs or knee-breeches. It is almost as rare in the Strand as it is in Market Street, Manchester. Cabinet Ministers and other sublime personages still wear it, coachmen still wear it, and my friend greasy-hat still wears it; but for the rest of us it is a splendour that is past, a memory of the world before the deluge.

It may be that it will revive. It would not be the first time that such a result of a great catastrophe was found to be only temporary. I remember that Pepys records in his Diary that one result of the Great Plague was that the wig went out of fashion. People were afraid to wear wigs that might be made of the hair of those who had died of infection. But the wig returned again for more than a century, though you may remember that in *The Rivals* there is an early hint of its final disappearance. There was never probably a more crazy fashion, and, like most crazy fashions, it began, as the "Alexandra limp" of our youth began, in snobbery. Was it not a fact that a bald-headed King wore a wig to conceal his baldness, which set all the flunkey-world wearing wigs to conceal their hair? This aping of the great is always converting some defect or folly into a virtue. When Lady Percy in *Henry IV* is lamenting Hotspur she says:—

... he was, indeed, the glass
Wherein the noble youth did dress themselves.
He had no legs that practised not his gait;
And speaking thick, which nature made his blemish,
Became the accents of the valiant;
For those that could speak low and tardily,
Would turn their own perfection to abuse.
To seem like him.

In the case of the top-hat the disappearance is due to the psychology of the war. The great tragedy has brought us down to the bed-rock of things and has made us feel somehow that ornament is out of place, and that the top-hat is a falsity in a world that has become a battlefield. I don't think women have shared this feeling to the same extent. I am told there were never so many sealskin coats to be seen as during last winter. But, perhaps, the women will say that men have been only too glad to use the war as an excuse for getting rid of an incubus. And they may be right. We had better not make too great a virtue of what is, after all, a comfortable change. Let us enjoy it without boasting.

Our enjoyment may be short-lived. We must not be surprised if this incredible hat returns in triumph with peace. It has survived the blasts of many centuries and infinite changes of fashion. It is, I suppose, the most ancient survival in the dress that men wear. There is in the Froissart collection at the British Museum an illumination (dating from the fifteenth century) showing the expedition of the French and English against the Barbary corsairs. And there seated in the boats are men clad in armour. They have put their helmets aside and are wearing top-hats! And it may be that when Macaulay's New Zealander, centuries hence, takes his seat on that broken arch of London Bridge to sketch the ruins of St. Paul's, he will sit under the shelter of a top-hat that has out-lasted all our greatness.

There must be some virtue in a thing that is so immortal. If the doctrine of the survival of the fittest applies to dress, it is the fittest thing we have. Trousers are a thing of yesterday with us, but our top-hat carries us back to the Wars of the Roses and beyond. It is not its beauty that explains it. I have never heard any one deny that it is ugly, though custom may have blunted our sense of its ugliness. It is not its utility. I have never heard any one claim that this strange cylinder had that quality. It is not its comfort

It is stiff, it is heavy, it is unmanageable in a wind and ruined by a shower of rain. It needs as much attention as a peevish child or a pet dog. It is not even cheap, and when it is disreputable it is the most disreputable thing on earth. What is the mystery of its strange persistence? Is it simply a habit that we cannot throw off or is there a certain snobbishness about it that appeals to the flunkeyism of men? That is perhaps the explanation. That is perhaps why it has disappeared when snobbishness is felt to be inconsistent with the world of stern realities and bitter sorrows in which we live. We are humble and serious and out of humour with the pretentious vanity of our top-hat.

ON LOSING ONE'S MEMORY

The case of the soldier in the Keighley Hospital who has lost his memory in the war and has been identified by rival families as a Scotchman, a Yorkshireman, and so on is one of the most singular personal incidents of the war. On the face of it it would seem impossible that a mother should not know her own son, or a brother his brother. Yet in this case it is clear that some of the claimants are mistaken. The incident is not, of course, without precedent. The most notorious case of the sort was that of Arthur Orton, the impudent Tichborne claimant, whose strongest card in his imposture was that Lady Tichborne believed him to be her long-lost son. In that case, no doubt, the maternal passion was the source of a credulity that blinded the old lady to the flagrant evidence of the fraud.

But, generally speaking, our memory of other faces is extremely vague and elusive. I have just come in from a walk with a friend of mine whom I have known intimately for many years. Yet for the life of me I could not at this moment tell you the colour of his eyes, nor could I give a reasonable account of his nose or of the shape of his face. I have a general sense of his appearance, but no absolute knowledge of the details, and if he were to meet me to-morrow with a blank stare and a shaven upper lip I should pass him without a thought of recognition.

Memory, in fact, is largely reciprocal, and when one of the parties has lost his power of response the key is gone. If the lock won't yield to the key, you are satisfied that the key is the wrong one, no matter how much it looks like the right one. I think I could tell my dog from a thousand other dogs; but if the creature were to lose his memory and to pass me in the street without answering my call, I should pass on, simply observing that he bore a remarkable likeness to my animal.

Most of us, I suppose, have experienced in a momentary and partial degree a sudden stoppage of the apparatus of memory. You are asked, let us say, to spell "parallelogram." In an ordinary way you could do it on your head or in your sleep; but the sudden demand gives you a mental jerk that makes the wretched word a hopeless chaos of r's and l's, and the more you try to sort them out the less convincing do they seem. Or walking with a friend you meet at a turn in the street that excellent woman, Mrs. Orpington-Smith. You know her as well as you know your own mother, but the fact that you have got to introduce her by her name forthwith sends her name flying into space. The passionate attempt to capture it before it escapes only makes its escape more certain, and you are reduced to the pitiful expedient of mumbling something that is inaudible.

The worst experience of a lapse of memory that ever came to me was in the midst of a speech which I had to make before a large gathering in a London hall. I had got to the middle of what I had to say when it seemed to me that the whole machine of the mind suddenly ceased to work. It was as though an immense loneliness descended on me. I saw the audience before me, but apart from vision I seemed bereft of all my faculties. If I had in that instant been asked for my name I am doubtful whether I could have got anywhere near it. Happily someone in a front row, thinking I was pausing for a word, threw out a suggestion. It was like magic. I felt the machine of memory start again with an almost audible "puff, puff," and I went on to the end quite comfortably. The pause had seemed terribly long to me, but I was surprised afterwards to find that it had been so brief as to be generally unnoticed or regarded as an artful way of emphasising a point. I let it go at that, but I knew myself that in that moment I had lost my memory.

Even distinguished and expert orators have been known to suffer from this absolute lapse of memory. The Rosebery incident–was it in the Chesterfield speech?–is perhaps the best known, but I once heard Mr. Redmond, the calmest and most assured of speakers, come to an *impasse* in the House of Commons that held him up literally for minutes.

We are creatures of memory, and when, as in the Keighley case, memory is gone personality itself has gone. Nothing is left but the empty envelope. The more fundamental functions of memory, the habits of respiration, of walking and physical movement, of mastication, and so on, remain. The Keighley man still eats and walks with all the knowledge of a lifetime. He probably preserves his taste for tobacco. But these things have nothing to do with personality. That is the product of the myriad mental impressions that you have stored up in your pilgrimage. There is not a moment in your life that is not charged with the significance of memory. You cannot hear the blackbird singing in the low bough in the evening without the secret music of summer eves long past being stirred within you. It is that response of the inner harp of memory that gives the song its beauty. And so everything we do and see and hear is touched with a thousand influences which we cannot catalogue, but which constitute our veritable selves. An old hymn tune, or an old song, a turn of phrase, a scent in the garden, a tone of voice, a curve in the path–everything comes to us weighted with its own treasures of memory, bitter or sweet, but always significant.

It is a mistake to suppose that memory is merely a capacity to remember facts. In that respect there is the widest diversity of experience. Macaulay could recite *Paradise Lost*, while Rossetti was a little doubtful whether the sun went round the earth or the earth round the sun. I once met an American elocutionist who could recite ten of Shakespeare's plays, and he showed me the wonderful system of mnemonics by which he achieved the miracle. But he was a mere recording machine–a dull fellow. The true argosy of memory is not facts, but a perfume compounded of all the sunsets we have ever seen, all the joys and friendships, pleasures and sorrows we have ever known, all the emotions we have felt, all the brave and mean things we have done, all the broken hopes we have suffered. To have lost that argosy is to be dead, no matter how healthy an appetite we retain.

ON WEARING A FUR-LINED COAT

A friend of mine—one of those people who talk about money with an air of familiarity that suggests that they have got an "out-crop" of the Rand reef in their back-gardens—said to me the other day that I ought to buy a fur-lined coat. There never was such a time as this for buying a fur-lined coat or a sealskin jacket, said he. What with the war, and the "sales," and the tradesmen's need of cash, they were simply being thrown at you. You could have them almost for the trouble of carrying them away. A trifle of fifteen or twenty pounds would buy one a coat that would be cheap at sixty guineas. And, remember, there was wear for twenty years in it. And think of the saving in doctor's bills—for you simply can't catch colds if you wear a fur coat. In short, not to buy a fur coat at this moment was an act of gross improvidence, a wrong to one's family, a ... a ... And then he looked, with the cold disapproval of a connoisseur, at the coat I was wearing. And in the light of that glance I saw for the first time that it was ... yes ... certainly, it was not what it had been.

Now I am not going to pretend that I have a soul above fur-lined coats. I haven't; I love them. And by fur coats I don't mean those adorned with astrakhan collars, which I abominate. A man in an astrakhan coat is to me a suspicious character, a stage baron, one who is probably deep in treasons, stratagems, and spoils. The suspicion is unjust to the gentleman in the astrakhan coat, of course. Most suspicions are unjust. And if you ask me to give reasons for this unreasoning hostility to astrakhan, I do not know that I could find them. Perhaps it is the dislike I have for artificial curls; perhaps it is that the astrakhan collar reminds me of those unhappy pet dogs who look as though they had been put in curl papers overnight and sent out into the streets by their owners as a poor jest. Yes, I think it must be that sense of artificiality which is at the root of the dislike. No doubt the curls are natural. No doubt the woolly sheep of Astrakhan do wear their coats in these little heaven-sent ringlets. But ... well ... "I do not like thee, Doctor Fell."

But fur-lined coats, with fine fur collars, are quite another affair. If I had the "magic nib," I could grow lyrical over them. I could, indeed. In place-of this article I would write an ode to a fur-lined coat. I would sing of the Asian wilds from whence it came, of its wondrous lines and its soft and silken texture, of its generous warmth and its caressing touch. I would set up such a universal hunger for fur coats that the tradesmen in Oxford Street and Regent Street would come and offer me a guinea a word to write advertisements for them.

And yet I shall not buy a fur-lined coat, and I will tell you why. A fur coat is not an article of clothing: it is a new way of life. You cannot say with reckless prodigality, "Here, I will have a fur coat and make an end of this gnawing passion." The fur coat is not an end: it is a beginning. You have got to live up to it. You have got to take the fur-coat point of view of your relations to society. When Chauncey Depew, as a boy, bought a beautiful spotted dog at a fair and took it home, the rain came down and the spots began to run into stripes. He took the dog back to the man of whom he had bought it and demanded an explanation. "But you had an umbrella with that dog," said the man. "No," said the boy. "Oh!" said the man, "there's an umbrella goes with that dog."

And so it is with the fur-lined coat. So many things "go with it." It is in this respect like that grand piano to which you succumbed in a moment of paternal weakness—or after a lucky stroke in rubber. The old furniture, which had seemed so unexceptionable before, suddenly became dowdy in the presence of this princely affair. You wanted new chairs and rugs and hangings to make the piano accord with its setting. Even the house fell under suspicion, and perhaps you date all your difficulties from the day that you bought that grand piano, and found that it had set you going on a new way of life just beyond your modest means.

If I bought a fur-lined coat I know that I should want to buy a motor-car to keep it company. It is possible, of course, to wear a fur coat in a motor-bus, but if you do you will assuredly have a sense that you are a little over-dressed, a trifle conspicuous, that the fellow-passengers are mentally remarking that such a coat ought to have a carriage of its own. It would provoke the comment that I heard the other night as two ladies in evening dress left a bus in a pouring rain. "Well," said one of the other lady passengers—a little enviously I thought, but still pertinently—"if I could afford to wear such fine clothes I think I would take a Cab." Yes, decidedly, the fur-lined coat would not be complete without the motor-car.

And then consider how it limits your freedom and raises the tariff against you. The tip that would be gratefully received if you were getting into that modest coat that you have discarded would be unworthy of the fur-lined standard that you have deliberately adopted. The recipient would take it frigidly, with a glance at the luxurious garment into which he had helped you—a glance that would cut you to the quick. Your friends would have to be fur-lined, too, and your dinners would no longer be the modest affairs of old, but would soar to the champagne standard. It would not be possible to slip unnoticed into your favourite little restaurant in Soho to take your simple chop, or to go in quest of that wonderful restaurant of Arne's of which "Aldebaran" keeps the secret. The modesty of Arne's would make you blush for your fur-lined coat.

"The genteel thing," said Tony Lumpkin's friend, "is the genteel thing at any time, if so be that a gentleman bees in a concatenation according-ly." That is it. The fur-lined coat is a genteel thing; but you have to be "in a concatenation according-ly." And there's the rub. It is not the coat, but its trimmings, so to speak, that give us pause. When you put on the coat you insensibly put off your old way of life. You set up a new standard, and have got to adapt your comings and goings, your habits and your expenditure to it. I once knew a man who had a fur-lined coat presented to him. It was a disaster. He could not live "in a concatenation according-ly." He lost his old friends without getting new ones. And his end ... Well, his end confirmed me in the conviction of the unwisdom of wearing a fur-lined coat before you are able, or disposed, to mould your life to the fur-lined standard.

IN PRAISE OF WALKING

I started out the other day from Keswick with a rucksack on my back, a Baddeley in my pocket, and a companion by my side. I like a companion when I go a-walking. "Give me a companion by the way," said Sterne, "if it be only to remark how the shadows lengthen as the sun declines." That is about enough. You do not want a talkative person. Walking is an occupation in itself. You may give yourself up to chatter at the beginning, but when you are warmed to the job you are disposed to silence, drop perhaps one behind the other, and reserve your talk for the inn table and the after-supper pipe. An occasional joke, an occasional stave of song, a necessary consultation over the map—that is enough for the way.

At the head of the Lake we got in a boat and rowed across Derwentwater to the tiny bay at the foot of Catbells. There we landed, shouldered our burdens, and set out over the mountains and the passes, and for a week we enjoyed the richest solitude this country can offer. We followed no cut-and-dried programme. I love to draw up programmes for a walking tour, but I love still better to break them. For one of the joys of walking is the sense of freedom it gives you. You are tied to no time-table, the slave of no road, the tributary of no man. If you like the road you follow it; if you choose the pass that is yours also; if your fancy (and your wind) is for the mountain tops, then over Great Gable and Scawfell, Robinson and Helvellyn be your way. Every short cut is for you, and every track is the path of adventure. The stream that tumbles down the mountain side is your wine cup. You kneel on the boulders, bend your head, and take such draughts as only the healthy thirst of the mountains can give. And then, on your way again singing:—

> Bed in the bush with the stars to see.
> Bread I dip in the river—
> There's the life for a man like me.
> There's the life for ever.

What liberty is there like this? You have cut your moorings from the world, you are far from telegraphs and newspapers and all the frenzies of the life you have left behind you, you are alone with the lonely hills and the wide sky and the elemental things that have been from the beginning and will outlast all the tortured drama of men. The very sounds of life—the whistle of the curlew, the bleating of the mountain sheep—add to the sense of primeval solitude. To these sounds the crags have echoed for a thousand and ten thousand years; to these sounds and to the rushing of the winds and the waters they will echo ten thousand years hence. It is as though you have passed out of time into eternity, where a thousand years are as one day. There is no calendar for this dateless world. The buzzard that you have startled from its pool in the gully and that circles round with wide-flapping wings has a lineage as ancient as the hills, and the vision of the pikes of Langdale that bursts on you as you reach the summit of Esk hause is the same vision that burst on the first savage who adventured into these wild fastnesses of the mountains.

And then as the sun begins to slope to the west you remember that, if you are among immortal things, you are only a mortal yourself, that you are getting footsore, and that you need a night's lodging and the comforts of an inn. Whither shall we turn? The valleys call us on every side. Newlands wide vale we can reach, or cheerful Borrowdale, or lonely Ennerdale, or—yes, to-night we will sup at Wastdale, at the jolly old inn that Auld Will Ritson used to keep, that inn sacred to the cragsman, where on New Year's Eve the gay company of climbers foregather from their brave deeds on the mountains and talk of hand-holds and foot-holds and sing the song of "The rope, the rope," and join in the chorus as the landlord trolls out:

> I'm not a climber, not a climber,
> Not a climber now,
> My weight is going fourteen stone—
> I'm not a climber now.

We shall not find Gaspard there to-night—Gaspard, the gay and intrepid guide from the Dauphiné, beloved of all who know the lonely inn at Wastdale. He is away on the battle-field fighting a sterner foe than the rocks and precipices of Great Gable and Scawfell. But Old Joe, the shepherd, will be there—Old Joe, who has never been in a train or seen a town and whose special glory is that he can pull uglier faces than any man in Cumberland. He will not pull them for anybody—only when he is in a good humour and for his cronies in the back parlour. To-night, perchance, we shall see his eyes roll as he roars out the chorus of "D'ye ken John Peel?" Yes, Wastdale shall be to-night's halt. And so over Black Sail, and down the rough mountain side to the inn whose white-washed walls hail us from afar out of the gathering shadows of the valley.

To-morrow? Well, to-morrow shall be as to-day. We will shoulder our rucksacks early, and be early on the mountains, for the first maxim in going a journey is the early start. Have the whip-hand of the day, and then you may loiter as you choose. If it is hot, you may bathe in the chill waters of those tarns that lie bare to the eye of heaven in the hollows of the hills—tarns with names of beauty and waters of such crystal purity as Killarney knows not. And at night we will come through the clouds down the wild course of Rosset Ghyll and sup and sleep in the hotel hard by Dungeon Ghyll, or, perchance, having the day well in hand, we will push on by Blea Tarn and Yewdale to Coniston, or by Easedale Tarn to Grasmere, and so to the Swan at the foot of Dunmail Raise. For we must call at the Swan. Was it not the Swan that Wordsworth's "Waggoner" so triumphantly passed? Was it not the Swan to which Sir Walter Scott used to go for his beer when he was staying with Wordsworth at Rydal Water? And behind the Swan is there not that fold in the hills where Wordsworth's "Michael" built, or tried to build, his sheepfold? Yes, we will stay at the Swan whatever befalls.

And so the jolly days go by, some wet, some fine, some a mixture of both, but all delightful, and we forget the day of the week, know no news except the changes in the weather and the track over the mountains, meet none of our kind except a rare vagabond like ourselves—with rope across his shoulder if he is a rock-man, with rucksack on back if he is a tourist—and with no goal save some far-off valley inn where we shall renew our strength and where the morrow's uprising to deeds shall be sweet.

I started to write in praise of walking, and I find I have written in praise of Lakeland. But indeed the two chants of praise are a single harmony, for I have written in vain if I have not shown that the way to see the most exquisite cabinet of beauties in this land is by the humble path of the pedestrian. He who rides through Lakeland knows nothing of its secrets, has tasted of none of its magic.

ON REWARDS AND RICHES

We have all been so occupied with the war in Europe that few of us, I suppose, have even heard of another war which has been raging in the law courts for 150 days or so between two South African corporations over some question of property. It seems to have been marked by a good deal of frightfulness. In the closing scenes Mr. Hughes, one of the counsel, complained that he had been called a fool, a liar, a scoundrel, and so on by his opponent, and the judge lamented that the case had been the occasion of so much barristerial bitterness.

But it was not the light which the case threw on the manners of counsel that interested me. After all, these things are part of the game. They have no more reality than the thumping blows which the Two Macs exchange in the pantomime. I have no doubt that after their memorable encounter in the Bardell *vs.* Pickwick case, Serjeant Buzfuz and Serjeant Snubbin went out arm-in-arm, and over their port in the Temple (where the wine is good and astonishingly cheap) made excellent fun of the whole affair. The wise juryman never takes any notice of the passion and tears, the heroics and the indignation of counsel. He knows that they are assumed not to enlighten but to darken his mind. I always recall in this connection the remark of a famous lawyer who rose to great eminence by the exercise of his emotions. He was standing by the graveside of a departed friend and observed that one of the mourners, a fellow–lawyer, was shedding real tears. "What a waste of raw material," he remarked in a whisper to his neighbour. "Those tears would be worth a guinea a drop before a jury."

What interested me in the case was the statement that the legal costs had been £150,000, and that Mr. Upjohn, K.C., alone had had a retainer of £1000, and had been kept going with a "refresher" of £100 a day. I like that word "refresher." It has a fine bibulous smack about it. Or perhaps it is a reminiscence of "the ring." Buzfuz feels a bit pumped by the day's round. He has perspired his £100, as it were, and is doubtful whether he can come up to the scratch without a refresher. And so he is taken to his corner by his client and dosed with another £100. Then all his ardour returns. He sees the thing as clear as daylight–the radiant innocence of the plaintiff, the black perfidy of the defendant. To-morrow evening the vision will have faded again, but another £100 will make it as plain as ever. Yes, it is a good word–"refresher"–a candid word, an honest word. It puts the relation on a sound business footing. There is no sham sentiment about it. Give me another refresher, says Buzfuz, and I'll shed another pailful of tears for you, and blacken both the defendant's eyes for him.

But as I read of these princely earnings I could not help thinking of what an irrational world this is in the matter of rewards. Here are a couple of lawyers hurling epithets and "cases" at each other at £100 a day. At the end a verdict is given for this side or that, and outside the people concerned no one is a penny the better or worse. And not many miles away hundreds of thousands of men are living in the mud of rat-infested trenches, with the sky raining destruction upon them, and death and mutilation the hourly incident of their lives. They have no retaining fee and no refresher. Their reward is a shilling a day, and it would take them 20,000 days to "earn" what one K.C. pockets each night. Could the mind conceive a more grotesque inversion of the law of services and rewards? You die for your country at a shilling a day, while at home Snubbin, K.C., is perspiring for his client at £100 a day.

This is old, cheap, and profitless stuff, you say. What is the good of drawing these contrasts? We know all about them. They are a part of the eternal inequality of things. Services and rewards never have had, and never will have, any relation to each other. Please do not remind us that Charlie Chaplin (or Charles Chaplin as he desires to be known) earns £130,000 a year by playing the fool in front of a camera, and that Wordsworth did not earn enough to keep himself in shoe-laces out of poetry which has become an immortal possession of humanity, and had to beg a noble nobody (the Earl of Lonsdale, I think) to get him a job as a stamp distributor to keep him in bread and butter.

Do not, my dear sir, be alarmed, I am not going to work that ancient theme off on you. And yet I think it is necessary sometimes to remind ourselves of these things. It is especially necessary now when there is so much easy talk about "equality of sacrifice," and so much easy forgetfulness of the inequality of rewards. It is useful, too, to remind ourselves that riches have no necessary relation to service. The genius for getting money is an altogether different thing from the genius for service. I suppose the Guinnesses (to take an example) are the richest people in Ireland. And I suppose Tom Kettle was one of the poorest. But who will dare apply the money test as the real measure of the values of these men to humanity—the one fabulously rich by brewing the "black stuff," as they call it in Ireland; the other glorious in his genius for spending himself, without a thought of return, on every noble cause and dying freely for liberty in the full tide of his powers? Which means the more to the world? Perhaps one effect of the war will be to give us a saner standard of values in these things—will teach us to look behind the money and title to the motives that get the money and the title. It is not the money and title we should distrust so much as the false implications attaching to them.

And, after all, we exaggerate the importance of the material rewards. They must often be very much of a bore. As the late Lord Salisbury once said, a man doesn't sleep any better because he has a choice of forty bedrooms in his house. He can only take one ride even though he has fifty motor-cars. He cannot get more joy out of the sunshine than you or I can. The birds sing and the buds swell for all of us, and in the great storehouse of natural delights there is no money taken and no price on the goods. Mr. Rockefeller's £100 a minute (if that is his income) is poor consolation for his bad digestion, and the late Mr. Pierpoint Morgan would probably have parted with half his millions to get rid of the excrescence that made his nose an unsightly joke. We cannot count our riches at the bank—even on the material side, much less on the spiritual. As I came along the village this morning I saw Jim Squire digging up his potatoes in the golden September light. I hailed him, and inquired how the crop was turning out. "A wunnerful fine crop," he said, "and thank the Lord, there ain't a spot o' disease in 'em." And as he straightened his back, pointed to the tubers strewn about him, and beamed like the sun at his good fortune, he looked the very picture of autumn's riches.

ON TASTE

I was in a feminine company the other day when the talk turned on war economies, with the inevitable allusion to the substitution of margarine for butter. I found it was generally agreed that the substitution had been a success. "Well," said one, "I bought some butter the other day–the sort we used to use–and put it on the table with the margarine which we have learned to eat. My husband took some, thinking it was margarine, made a wry face, and said, 'It won't do. This margarine economy is beyond me. We must return to butter, even if we lose the war.' I explained to him that he was eating butter, *the* butter, and he said, 'Well, I'm hanged!' Now, what do you think of that?"

I said I thought it showed that taste was a matter of habit, and that imagination played a larger part in our make-up than we supposed. We say of this or that thing that it is "an acquired taste," as though the fact was unusual, whereas the fact would seem to be that we dislike most things until we have habituated ourselves to them. As a youth I abominated the taste of tobacco. It was only by an industrious apprenticeship to the herb that I overcame my natural dislike and got to be its obedient servant. And even my taste here is unstable. I needed a certain tobacco to be happy and thought there was no other tobacco like it. But I discovered that was all nonsense. When the war tax sent the price up, I determined that my expenditure should not go up with it, and I tried a cheaper sort. I found it distasteful at first, but now I prefer it to my old brand, just as the lady's husband finds that he prefers the new margarine to the old butter.

And it is not only gastronomic taste which seems so much the subject of habit. That hat that was so absolute a thing last year is as dowdy and impossible to-day as if it had been the fashion of the Babylonians. It has always been so. "We had scarce worn cloth one year at the Court," says Montaigne, "what time we mourned for our King Henrie the Second, but certainly in every man's opinion all manner of silks were already become so vile and abject that was any man seen to wear them he was presently judged to be some countrie fellow or mechanical man." And you remember that in Utopia gold was held of so small account by comparison with iron that it was used for the baser purposes of the household.

We are adaptable creatures, and easily make our tastes conform to our environment and our customs. There are certain savage tribes who wear rings through their noses. When Mrs. Brown, of Tooting, sees pictures of them she remarks to Mr. Brown on the strange habits of these barbarous people. And Mr. Brown, if he has a touch of humour in him, points to the rings hanging from Mrs. Brown's ears, and says: "But, my dear, why is it barbarous to wear a ring in the nostril and civilised to wear rings in the ears?" The dilemma is not unlike that of the savage tribe whom the Greeks induced to give up cannibalism. But when the cannibals, who had piously eaten their parents, were asked instead to adopt the Greek custom of burning the bodies they were horrified at the suggestion. They would cease to eat them; but burn them? No. I can imagine Mrs. Brown's savages agreeing to take the rings out of their noses, but refusing blankly to put them in their ears.

I have no doubt that the long-haired Cavaliers used to regard the short hair of the Puritans as the "limit" in bad taste, but the man who today dares to walk down the Strand with hair streaming down his back is looked at as a curiosity and a crank, and we all join in that delightful addition to the Litany which Moody invented: "From long-haired men and short-haired women, Good Lord, deliver us." But who shall say that our children will not reverse the prayer?

Even in my own brief span I have seen men's faces pass through every hirsute change under the Protean influence of "good taste." I remember when, to be really a student of good form, a man wore long side-whiskers of the Dundreary type. Then "mutton chops" and a moustache were the thing; then only a moustache; now we have got back to the Romans and the clean shave. But where is the absolute "good taste" in all this? Or take trousers. If you had lived a hundred years ago and had dared to go about in trousers instead of knee-breeches you would have been written down a vulgar fellow. Even the great Duke of Wellington in 1814 was refused admittance to Almack's because he presented himself in trousers. Now we relegate knee-breeches to fancy dress balls and Court functions.

But sometimes the canons of good taste are astonishingly irrational. Who was it who set Christendom wearing black, sad, hopeless black as the symbol of mourning? The Roman ladies, who had never heard of the doctrine of the Resurrection, clothed themselves in white for mourning. It is left for the Christian world, which looks beyond the grave, to wear the habiliments of despair. If I go to a funeral I am as conventional as anybody else, for I have not the courage of a distinguished statesman whom I saw at his brother's funeral wearing a blue overcoat, check trousers, and a grey waistcoat, and carrying a green umbrella. I can give you his name if you doubt me—a great name, too. And he would not deny the impeachment. I am not prepared to endorse his idea of good taste; but I hate black. "Why should I wear black for the guests of God?" asked Ruskin. And there is no answer. Perhaps among the consequences of the war there will be a repudiation of this false code of taste.

ON A HAWTHORN HEDGE

As I turned into the lane that climbs the hillside to the cottage under the high beech woods I was conscious of a sort of mild expectation that I could not explain. It was late evening. Venus, who looks down with such calm splendour upon this troubled earth in these summer nights, had disappeared, but the moon had not yet risen. The air was heavy with those rich odours which seem so much more pungent by night than by day—those odours of summer eves that Keats has fixed for ever in the imagination:–

> I cannot see what flowers are at my feet.
> Nor what soft incense hangs upon the boughs;
> But, in embalmed darkness, guess each sweet
> Wherewith the seasonable month endows
> The grass, the thicket, and the fruit-tree wild;
> White hawthorn....

Ah, that was it. I remembered now. A fortnight ago, when I last came up this lane by night, it was the flash of the white hawthorn in the starlight that burst upon me with such a sudden beauty. I knew the spot. It was just beyond here, where the tall hedgerow leans over the grass side-track and makes a green arbour by the wayside. I should come to it in a minute or two, and catch once more that ecstasy of spring.

And when I reached the spot the white hawthorn had vanished. The arbour was there, but its glory had faded. The two weeks I had spent in Fleet Street had stripped it of its crown, and the whole pageant of the year must pass before I could again experience that sudden delight of the hedgerows bursting into foam. I do not mind confessing that I continued my way up the lane with something less than my former exhilaration. Partly no doubt this was due to the fact that the hill at this point begins its job of climbing in earnest, and is a stiff pull at the end of a long day's work and a tiresome journey—especially if you are carrying a bag.

But the real reason of the slight shadow that had fallen on my spirit was the vanished hawthorn. Poor sentimentalist, you say, to cherish these idle fancies in this stern world of blood and tears. Well, perhaps it is this stern world of blood and tears that gives these idle fancies their poignancy. Perhaps it is through those fancies that one feels the transitoriness of other things. The coming and the parting in the round of nature are so wonderfully mingled that we can never be quite sure whether the joy of the one triumphs over the regret for the other. It is always "Hail" and "Farewell" in one breath. I heard the cuckoo calling across the meadows to-day, and already I noticed a faltering in his second note. Soon the second note will be silent altogether, and the single call will sound over the valley like the curfew bell of spring.

Who, I thought, would not fix these fleeting moments of beauty if he could? Who would not keep the cuckoo's twin shout floating for ever over summer fields and the blackbird for ever fluting his thanksgiving after summer showers? Who can see the daffodils nodding their heads in sprightly dance without sharing the mood of Herrick's immortal lament that that dance should be so brief:—

> Fair daffodils, we weep to see
> You haste away so soon;
> As yet the early-rising sun
> Has not attain'd its noon.
> Stay, stay.
> Until the hasting day
> Has run
> But to the evensong;
> And, having prayed together, we
> Will go with you along.

Yes, I think Herrick would have forgiven me for that momentary lapse into regretfulness over the white hawthorn. He would have understood. You will see that he understood if you will recall the second stanza, which, if you are the person I take you for, you will do without needing to turn to a book.

It is the same sense of the transience of beauty that inspired the "Ode to a Grecian Urn" on which pastoral beauty was fixed in eternal rapture:—

> Ah, happy, happy boughs I that cannot shed
> Your leaves, nor ever bid the spring adieu.

And there we touch the paradox of this strange life. We would keep the fleeting beauty of Nature, and yet we would not keep it. The thought of those trees whose leaves are never shed, and of that eternal spring to which we never bid adieu, is pleasant to toy with, but after all we would not have it so. It is no more seriously tenable than the thought that little Johnny there should remain forever at the age of ten. You may feel that you would like him to remain at the age of ten. Indeed you are a strange parent if you do not look back a little wistfully to the childhood of your children, and wish you could see them as you once saw them. But you would not really have Johnny stick at ten. After five years of the experience you would wish little Johnny dead. For life and its beauty are a living thing, and not a pretty fancy sculptured on a Grecian urn.

And so with the pageant of Nature. If the pageant stopped, the wonder itself would stop. I should have no sudden shock of delight at hearing the first call of the cuckoo in spring or seeing my hawthorn hedge burst into snowy blossoms. I should no longer remark the jolly clatter of the rooks in the February trees which forms the prologue of spring, nor look out for the coming of the first primrose or the arrival of the first swallow. I should cease, it is true, to have the pangs of "Farewell," but I should cease also to have the ecstasy of "Hail." I should have my Grecian urn, but I should have lost the magic of the living world.

By the time I had reached the gate I had buried my regrets for the vanished hawthorn. I knew that to-morrow I should find new miracles in the hedgerows—the wild rose and the honeysuckle, and after them the blackberries, and after these again the bright-hued hips and haws. And though the cuckoo's note should fail him, there would remain the thrush, and after the thrush that constant little fellow in the red waistcoat would keep the song going through the dark winter days.

www.ingramcontent.com/pod-product-compliance
Lightning Source LLC
Chambersburg PA
CBHW081656270326
41933CB00017B/3188

* 9 781603 862547 *